Otis Frederick Reed Waite

Vermont in the Great Rebellion

Containing historical and biographical sketches

Otis Frederick Reed Waite

Vermont in the Great Rebellion
Containing historical and biographical sketches

ISBN/EAN: 9783337216641

Printed in Europe, USA, Canada, Australia, Japan

Cover: Foto ©ninafisch / pixelio.de

More available books at **www.hansebooks.com**

VERMONT

IN THE

GREAT REBELLION.

CONTAINING

HISTORICAL AND BIOGRAPHICAL SKETCHES, Etc.

BY

MAJ. OTIS F. R. WAITE.

CLAREMONT, N.H.:
TRACY, CHASE AND COMPANY.
1869.

TO THE

WIVES, MOTHERS AND SISTERS

OF THE

BRAVE OFFICERS AND MEN

WHO WERE IN THE WAR OF THE REBELLION

FROM THE

STATE OF VERMONT

THIS BOOK IS REVERENTLY INSCRIBED,

BY THE AUTHOR.

PREFACE.

A POPULAR writer has said, "Not a day passes over the earth but men and women of no note do great deeds, speak great words, and suffer noble sorrows. Of these obscure heroes, philosophers and martyrs, the greater part will never be known till the hour when many that were great shall be small, and the small great; but of others, the world's knowledge may be said to sleep; their lives and characters lie hidden from nations in the annals that record them."

In presenting to the public a book of this size, it would be but folly to claim that it gives anything like a full history of the noble and self-sacrificing acts and gallant conduct of the Vermont troops, during the four years that they were engaged in the War of the Rebellion. Many of their most noteworthy deeds will never have a public record. They must forever remain the sacred property of those who enacted them. Hundreds of noble men, entitled to the highest meed of praise, and the greatest gratitude of their fellow-statesmen, will be counted with the unnumbered host whose unnoticed sufferings and toils, in field and camp, form always the material out of which military glory comes to the few.

The author, in preparing this work, has aimed to convey an idea of the camp, garrison and picket duty performed, and the battles fought, by the several regiments and companies which went to the field from Vermont. To do this he has availed himself freely of the Adjutant and Inspector General's records and reports, covering the period of the war, — without which an attempt to prepare a book like this must have proved abortive.

Biographical notices are given of a few only of the many deserving men who took prominent parts in the great tragic drama put upon the stage by the deluded people of a section of the country; while there remain hundreds, and perhaps thousands, entitled to the same especial consideration, whose record could not be obtained by ordinary means.

The book is submitted with the hope that the veil of charity will be thrown over its short-comings and imperfections.

O. F. R. W.

June, 1869.

INDEX.

	PAGE
THE REBELLION,	9
ACTION OF VERMONT,	56
VERMONT TROOPS,	94
VERMONT BRIGADE,	116
SECOND VERMONT BRIGADE,	216

REGIMENTS. — First, ... 58, 106
Second, ... 61, 117
Third, ... 62, 118
Fourth, ... 64, 118
Fifth, ... 65, 118
Sixth, ... 67, 119
Seventh, ... 68, 196
Eighth, ... 70, 203
Ninth, ... 75, 205
Tenth, ... 77, 210
Eleventh, ... 77, 215
Twelfth, ... 86, 216
Thirteenth, ... 87, 216
Fourteenth, ... 88, 216
Fifteenth, ... 89, 216
Sixteenth, ... 90, 216
Seventeenth, ... 230

SHARPSHOOTERS. — First Company, ... 72, 235
Second do., ... 72, 235
Third do., ... 73, 235

BATTERIES. — First, ... 71, 238
Second, ... 72, 239
Third, ... 240

INDEX.

	PAGE.
CAVALRY. — First Regiment,	73, 242

BATTLES. — Antietam, ... 142
          Cedar Creek, ... 185
          Crampton's Gap, ... 139
          Fredericksburg, ... 146, 149
          Gettysburg, ... 164, 217
          Goulding's Farm, ... 128, 130
          Lee's Mills, ... 120
          Petersburg, ... 179
          Rappahannock Station, ... 167
          Savage's Station, ... 131
          White Oak Swamp, ... 133
          Wilderness, ... 168
          Williamsburg, ... 126

BIOGRAPHICAL. — Brown, Lieut. Col. Addison, Jr. . . . 269
                  Cummings, Lieut. Col. Charles, . . 261
                  Farr, Captain Dennie W., ... 271
                  Jarvis, Major Charles, ... 265
                  Phelps, General John Wolcott, . . 259
                  Stannard, General George J., . . . 251
                  Tyler, Colonel John Steele, . . . 263
                  Wales, Brevet Major Elijah, . . . 267
                  Washburn, General Peter T., . . . 256

INCIDENTS. — Before the Battle of Bethel, ... 273
            Bravery at Lee's Mills, ... 278
            Dying Soldier's Prayer for Pres't Lincoln, 281
            Escaped Prisoners, ... 280
            Last Words of Colonel Stone, ... 277
            A Slave's Prayer, ... 279

ANECDOTES. — Don't See It, ... 288
             Drummer Boy, ... 287
             Heroism at Fredericksburg, ... 287

THE REBELLION.

FROM the day of the adoption of the Constitution of the United States there has been an antagonism between the Northern and the Southern portions of the Union. That Constitution contains not one word hostile to liberty and humanity. In it, however, is a single phrase which has been interpreted differently by the different sections of the country — "held to labor." At the North, these simple, harmless words mean a hired man, an apprentice. At the South, they mean a slave, feudal bondage, the right of property in man, and all the attendant oppressions and cruelties. From these different constructions of the spirit of the organic law of the country, and the widely-different modes of life and of thought, the antagonism between the North and the South has grown with the growth and strengthened with the strength of the nation. Mr. Iverson, of Georgia, in speaking on this subject in the United States Senate, on the 5th of December, 1860, said, "Sir, disguise the fact as you will, there is an enmity between the Northern and the Southern people, which is deep and enduring, and you never can eradicate it — never. . We are enemies as much as if we were hostile States. We have not lived in peace. We are not now living in peace. It is not expected that we shall ever live in peace."

Mr. Mason, of Virginia, in the same debate, said, "This is a war of sentiment and opinion, by one form of society against another form of society."

Garrett Davis, senator from Kentucky, said, "The Cotton States, by their slave labor, have become wealthy, and many of their planters have princely revenues — from fifty thousand to one hundred thousand dollars a year. This wealth has begot pride, and insolence, and ambition; and those points of the Southern character have been displayed most insultingly in the halls of Congress. As a class, the wealthy cotton growers are insolent, they are proud, they are domineering, they are ambitious. They have monopolized the government in its honors for forty or fifty years, with few interruptions. When they saw the scepter about to depart from them, in the election of Abraham Lincoln, sooner than give up office, and the spoils of office, in their mad and wicked ambition, they determined to disrupt the old Confederation, and erect a new one, wherein they would have undisputed power. Nine out of ten of the Northern people were sound upon the subject. They were opposed to the extension of slavery; and I do not condemn them for that: but they were willing to accord to the slaveholders all their constitutional rights."

The slaveholders had become arrogant in their demands upon Congress, claiming that the Constitution favored freedom, free labor, and free schools, and that it should be so far changed as to maintain the exclusive claims of an aristocratic class, and to strengthen their hold upon their slaves. They insisted that the domestic slave trade should be nurtured, and the foreign slave trade opened. They demanded the right to extend slavery over all the Territories of the United States; the right to hold their slaves in all the States of the Union temporarily; that speaking or writing against slavery in any State of the Union should be a penal offence; that the North should catch their fugitive slaves, and send them back to bondage; and that the administration of the General Government should be placed in the hands of those only whom the South could trust, as the pledged enemies of republican equality, and the friends of slavery. These were the demands of the South, which, they said, must be acceded to, or they would dash the Union to pieces and from the fragments construct a Confederacy, with slavery for its corner-stone.

In the election of Abraham Lincoln to the Presidency, in 1860, the people of the United States said, most emphatically, "We will not accede to these arrogant and wicked demands. We will not thus change the Constitution of our fathers. We will abide by it as it is." In an appeal to the ballot-box the slaveholders were fairly and overwhelmingly defeated, and they determined to secede and break up the Union.

As long ago as 1856, Hon. Preston Brooks, of South Carolina, said, in a speech in Charleston, at an ovation given in his honor, for his brutal assault upon Senator Sumner, of Massachusetts, for words spoken in debate in his place in the Senate, "I tell you, fellow-citizens, from the bottom of my heart, that the only mode which I think available for meeting it [the issue], is just to tear the Constitution of the United States, trample it under foot, and form a Southern Confederacy, every State of which shall be a Slaveholding State."

Mr. Hunter, of Virginia, detailed in the Senate of the United States the changes in the Constitution with which alone the Slaveholders would be satisfied. His demands were, —

1. Congress shall have no power to abolish slavery

in the States, or the District of Columbia, or the dockyards, forts, and arsenals of the United States.

2. Congress shall not abolish, tax, or obstruct the slave trade between the States.

3. It shall be the duty of each of the States to suppress combination, within its jurisdiction, for the armed invasion of any other State.

4. States shall be admitted with or without slavery, according to the election of the people.

5. It shall be the duty of the States to restore fugitive slaves, or pay the value of the same.

6. Fugitives from justice shall be deemed those who have offended the laws of the State within its jurisdiction, and shall have escaped therefrom.

7. Congress shall recognize and protect as property, what is held to be such by the laws of any State, in the Territories, dockyards, arsenals, forts, and wherever the United States have exclusive jurisdiction.

'Mr. Hunter also demanded that there should always be two Presidents chosen, one by the Slaveholding States, and the other by the North, and that no act should be valid unless approved by both Presidents. Thus giving to not more than three hundred thousand slaveholders as much power in the government as to the other thirty millions of population. He also demanded that the United States Supreme Court should consist of ten members, five to be chosen by the little handful of slaveholders, and the other five by the millions of freemen.

To accomplish their purpose, every man at the South was to be compelled, by the reign of terror, to support the cause of the slaveholders. Vigilance committees were organized, the mails were searched, and a system of espionage introduced, such as no despotism on earth ever before equalled. A gentleman from Hinds County, Mississippi, wrote to the editor of the New York Tribune, under date of February 7, 1861, —

"I have lived in this State twenty-five years. Yet if I should say, not openly upon the housetop, but at my own table, among my family and friends congregated there, that I do not consider that the South has any real grievance to complain of, and totally oppose the secession of this or any other State from the Union, my property, my life even, would not be safe an hour. It is very certain that those who are in favor of secession have no more than a bare majority in any of the Southern States. We, the Union men of the South, call on you of the North not to desert us."

The slaveholders demanded further, in addition to the right of the general extension of slavery, that the laws of the Free States should be so changed as to enable them to hold their enslaved servants at the North temporarily, while, at the same time, they refused to allow a Northern gentleman even to enter their States with a free hired colored servant.

The candidates for President in 1860 were Abraham Lincoln, of Illinois, nominated by the Republican party, who was openly pledged to resist the extension of slavery, while he avowed that Congress had no constitutional right to interfere with slavery in those States where it existed, but that it was both the right and the duty of Congress to prohibit slavery in all the United States Territories. John C. Breckinridge was the candidate of the slaveholders, pledged to administer the government in the most effectual way to nurture, and to give increasing political power to the institution of slavery. Stephen A. Douglas and John Bell were supported by those who wished to effect some compromise, and who were ready, for the sake of avoiding civil war, to make very great concessions to the South.

The election took place on the 6th of November, and the result of the popular vote was, for electors: Lincoln, 1,857,610; Douglas, 1,365,976; Breckinridge, 847,953; Bell, 591,613; giving Lincoln the electoral votes of seventeen out of the thirty-three States; eleven for Breckinridge; three for Bell, and one — Missouri — with three-sevenths of New Jersey, for Douglas.

Mr. Lincoln received the electoral votes of California, 4; Connecticut, 6; Illinois, 11; Indiana, 13; Iowa, 4; Maine, 8; Massachusetts, 13; Michigan, 6; Minnesota, 4; New Hampshire, 5; New Jersey, 4; New York, 35; Ohio, 23; Oregon, 3; Pennsylvania, 27; Rhode Island, 4; Vermont, 5; Wisconsin, 5 — 180. John C. Breckinridge received the votes of Alabama, 9; Arkansas, 4; Delaware, 3; Florida, 3; Georgia, 10; Louisiana, 6; Maryland, 8; Mississippi, 7; North Carolina, 10; South Carolina, 8; Texas, 4 — 72. Stephen A. Douglas received the votes of Missouri, 9, and 3 of the 7 votes of New Jersey — 12. John Bell received the votes of Kentucky, 12; Tennessee, 12; Virginia, 15 — 39. Hannibal Hamlin, of Maine, was elected Vice-President, receiving 180 electoral votes, while Joseph Lane received 72, Edward Everett 39, and Herschel Johnson 12. The electors chosen in Vermont were, William Henry, Henry G. Root, Joseph Warner, Edward A. Cahoon, and D. W. C. Clark.

On the fifteenth of February, in the presence of the two Houses of Congress, the Electoral votes were officially counted and declared by John C. Breckinridge, the slaveholders' candidate for President, who was at that time Vice-President and the President of the Senate. Amid deadly silence, the result was announced as follows: One hundred and eighty votes were cast for Abraham Lincoln; seventy-two for John C. Breckinridge; thirty-nine for John Bell; twelve for Stephen A. Douglas. This gave to Abraham

Lincoln a majority of fifty-seven votes over all the other candidates. Whereupon the Vice-President rising, said, "Abraham Lincoln, of Illinois, having received a majority of the whole number of electoral votes, is duly elected President of the United States for the four years commencing on the 4th of March, 1861. And Hannibal Hamlin, of Maine, having received a majority of the whole number of electoral votes, is duly elected Vice-President for the same term."

This was a day of great excitement in Washington. It was a slaveholding city, in the midst of slaveholding States, and fire-eaters from the South were there in great numbers, and had boldly threatened that the announcement of the vote for President should not be made, and that the government should be broken up in a row. James Buchanan was then President; had been intimidated by the slaveholders, and, if he had not been made their tool, had not the courage to prepare to meet and thwart their threats of violence. In that crisis the nation could place but little reliance upon his efficiency, and reposed but little confidence in his patriotism. General Winfield Scott had prepared to meet any emergency that might arise, by drawing to the city a military force so planting their guns as to sweep the streets at the first outbreak, thus overawing the conspirators; and the day passed quietly, and everything was done with decency and in order.

On the 20th of December, 1860, a convention of a few score of slaveholders in South Carolina led off in the rebellion, and passed the following resolution: —

"We, the people of the State of South Carolina, in convention assembled, do declare and ordain, and it is hereby declared and ordained, that the ordinance adopted by us in convention, on the 23d of May, in the year of our Lord 1788, whereby the Constitution of the United States of America was ratified, and also all acts, and parts of acts, of the General Assembly of this State ratifying the amendments of said Constitution, are hereby repealed, and that the Union now subsisting between South Carolina and other States, under the name of the United States of America, is hereby dissolved."

In the course of the month of January, 1861, the States of Alabama, Florida, Georgia, Louisiana, Mississippi, and North Carolina followed, and adopted similar acts of secession to that adopted by South Carolina; and, on the 4th of February, forty-two delegates, representing these seven seceded States, met at Montgomery, Alabama, and proceeded to organize a Southern Confederacy of these, with such others as might subsequently be added, and elected Jefferson Davis, President, and Alexander H. Stephens,

Vice-President. On the 18th of the same month, Jefferson Davis was inaugurated President at Montgomery.

President Buchanan's cabinet was composed of slaveholders, and Northern men with Southern principles. In November, as soon as the result of the presidential election was known, these men set at work to embarrass and cripple the government, that its capital, forts, arsenals, public property, and munitions of war might easily fall into the hands of the wicked conspirators against the Union. Lewis Cass, of Michigan, was Secretary of State, and tried to persuade the President to take steps to avert the impending calamity, and protect the public property; failing in which, he resigned in December, and was succeeded by Jeremiah S. Black, of Pennsylvania. Howell Cobb, a slaveholder from Georgia, was Secretary of the Treasury. When he entered upon office, the national treasury was in a healthy and prosperous condition. He resigned, and took an office under the conspirators. More than six millions of dollars had been stolen, and, when his successor went into office, the treasury was on the verge of bankruptcy. Jacob Thompson, a Mississippi slaveholder, was Secretary of the Interior, and did all in his power to aid the conspirators. John B. Floyd, a Virginia slaveholder, was Secretary of War.

There was a plan on foot — which, thank God, was discovered in season to thwart it — to assassinate the President elect when on his way to Washington to take his seat. In the panic, which it was supposed would ensue, troops from the adjacent Slave States of Maryland and Virginia were to seize upon Washington and all its treasures, and make it the capital of the new Confederacy. To this end the United States army — but a few thousands in number — was so disposed that the soldiers could not rally to the support of the government, while the arsenals at the North were despoiled, the arms sent to the Slave States, and the fortifications in those States seized and garrisoned by the conspirators. Having accomplished all this, Floyd sent in his resignation, joined the rebels, and was appointed a general in their army. Most of the clerks and employees in the different departments of the government at Washington were in sympathy with the conspirators, and many were actively aiding them in their damnable plots to overthrow the best government that the sun ever shone upon.

Isaac Toucey, of Connecticut, — a Northern man with Southern principles, — was Secretary of the Navy. According to the report of his successor to Congress, July 4, 1861, our fleet in February, 1861, consisted of ninety vessels of all classes, carrying two thousand four hundred and fifteen guns; and was manned by a complement of about seven thousand six hundred men, exclusive of officers and marines. Notwithstanding the necessity for the presence of this fleet in our own waters to aid the government in this trying hour, it was dispersed, for no good excuse; the Brooklyn, twenty-five guns, and the storeship Relief, two guns, only remaining, to defend the entire Atlantic coast.

On the 21st of February, 1861, a select committee of five, appointed by the House of Representatives, in a report upon the conduct of the Secretary of the Navy, after stating what disposition had been made of our naval force, say, —

"The committee cannot fail to call attention to this extraordinary disposition of the entire naval force of the country, and especially in connection with the present no less extraordinary and critical juncture of our political affairs. They cannot call to mind any period in the past history of the country, of such profound peace and internal repose, as would justify so entire an abandonment of the coast of the country to the chance of fortune. Certainly since the nation possessed a navy, it has never before sent its entire available force into distant seas, and exposed the immense interests at home, of which it is the especial guardian, to the dangers from which, even in times of the utmost quiet, prudence and forecast do not always shelter them.

"To the committee this disposition of the naval force, at this most critical period, seems extraordinary. The permitting of vessels to depart for distant seas after these unhappy difficulties had broken out at home, the omission to put in repair and commission, ready for orders, a single one of the twenty-eight ships dismantled and unfit for service, in our own ports, and that, too, while $646,639.79 of the appropriation for repairs in the navy, the present year, remained unexpended, were, in the opinion of the committee, grave errors, without justification or excuse."

All these, and many other like wicked acts, were being committed under the eye and with the knowledge of President Buchanan, and by officers whom he had the power to displace at any moment, and yet he never raised his hand to prevent or check them.

There were a few leading and influential men in the slave States, slaveholders themselves, who, wiser than the rest, were opposed to secession and the disruption of the old Union, but were soon forced to acquiesce in the schemes and movements of the conspirators. They were whipped into the ranks of the rebellion. It was not sufficient for them to remain silent or neutral, but they must be active for treason, or their property and lives were at the mercy of a set of fiends who showed no mercy.

Alexander H. Stephens, for many years a member of the United States House of Representatives from Georgia, and one of the most influential men in that State, opposed secession. In a speech to an immense gathering of his constituents at Milledgeville, on the 14th of November, 1860, he said, —

"The first question that presents itself is, Shall the people of the South secede from the Union in consequence of the election of Mr. Lincoln to the Presidency of the United States? My countrymen, I tell you frankly, candidly, and earnestly, that I do not think that they ought. In my judgment, the election of no man, constitutionally chosen to that high office, is sufficient cause for any State to separate from the Union. It ought to stand by, and aid still in maintaining the Constitution of the country. To make a point of resistance to the government, to withdraw from it, because a man has been constitutionally elected, puts us in the wrong. We are pledged to maintain the Constitution. Many of us have sworn to support it. Can we, therefore, for the mere election of a man to the Presidency, and that, too, in accordance with the prescribed forms of the Constitution, make a point of resistance to the government, without becoming the breakers of that sacred instrument ourselves?

"But that this government of our fathers, with

all its defects, comes nearer the objects of all good governments than any other on the face of the earth, is my settled conviction. Contrast it now with any other on the face of the earth. (England, said Mr. Toombs.) England, my friend says. Well, that is the next best, I grant; but I think we have improved upon England. Statesmen tried their apprentice hand on the government of England, and then ours was made. Ours sprung from that, avoiding many of its defects, taking most of the good, and leaving out many of its errors, and, from the whole, constructing and building up this model republic — the best which the history of the world gives any account of. Where will you go, following the sun in its circuit around our globe, to find a government that better protects the liberties of its people, and secures to them the blessings we enjoy? I think that one of the evils that beset us is a surfeit of liberty, an exuberance of the priceless blessings for which we are ungrateful.

"I look upon this country, with our institutions, as the Eden of the world — the paradise of the universe. It *may be* that out of it we may become greater and more prosperous; but I am candid and sincere in telling you that I fear, if we rashly evince passion, and without sufficient cause shall take that step, that, instead of becoming greater and more powerful, prosperous, and happy, — instead of becoming gods, we will become demons, and at no distant day commence cutting one another's throats."

Early in January, 1861, Georgia passed an act of secession, and joined the other States that had withdrawn from the Union; and in February, Mr. Stephens accepted the office of Vice-President of the new Confederacy, and traversed the Slave States, and exerted all his powers to rouse the people to war against the government of the United States.

The first plan of the rebels was to break up the government of the United States, take possession of its capital, navy yards, armories, arsenals, and fortifications, preparatory for the outbreak. When all this was done it was supposed there would be but a feeble resistance on the part of the people of the North. The government was to be reorganized, with slavery established in all the States and Territories, and Jefferson Davis as its head. All arrangements for carrying out this scheme had been deliberately and carefully made, and were apparently near consummation, before the people of the North could be made to comprehend the possibility of such a movement by any considerable portion of the people of the Slave States.

One part of this most wicked and damnable plot was to assassinate President Lincoln as he passed through Baltimore, on his way to Washington, to be inaugurated. It was discovered in season, however, to prevent such a great calamity to the country. At all the cities and large towns on his route the people assembled and gave him most enthusiastic receptions. The loyal people of Baltimore had made preparations to testify their respect by a large gathering, procession, &c., while the conspirators had arranged to get up a riot at the depot, on his arrival, during which the President, unarmed and unprotected, was to be stabbed or shot. This plan was discovered by the police, who informed General Scott and senator Seward, and Frederick W Seward, son of the senator, was immediately despatched to meet the President, and inform him of the danger to his life. He had a public reception at Harrisburg, after which, with a few of his friends, he retired to his private apartments at the hotel about six o'clock in the evening, and as he was known to be weary, was not interrupted. As soon as it was dark, he, in company with Colonel Lamon, unobserved, entered a hack and drove to the Pennsylvania railroad, where a special train was waiting for him. The telegraph wires were in the mean time cut, so that the knowledge of his departure, if discovered or suspected, could not be sent abroad. The train reached Philadelphia at half past ten o'clock that night. They drove immediately across the city to the Baltimore and Washington depot. The regular night train was just leaving, at a quarter past eleven. They took berths in a sleeping-car, and, without any change, passed directly through Baltimore, and arrived at Washington safely and unexpectedly, at half past six o'clock next morning, being the 23d of February. Thus was an important part of the scheme of the rebels frustrated, and the proposed attempt to seize the capital was prevented by the energy and watchfulness of the friends of the incoming administration.

The conspirators had counted on a divided North, believing there were many friends of their cherished institution here who would join them in their rebellion against the government. Here, again, they made a great mistake; for, when the people of the Free States were aware of the wicked plot to break up the Union, and the extent of it, they arose as one man to meet the emergency; and the Northern men, with Southern sympathies, found themselves in a most disgraceful and hopeless minority. And the plan to invade the Northern States had to be abandoned, while General Scott, contrary to the wish of President Buchanan, who was completely under control of the slave power, had gathered about three hundred troops in and about the capital for its protection.

On the retirement of the traitor Floyd from the

War Department, Hon. Joseph Holt, of Kentucky, was appointed to fill the place. He coöperated with General Scott in the adoption of vigorous measures for the protection of Washington from the menaced capture by the rebels, which greatly alarmed them. On the 18th of February, Mr. Holt addressed a letter to President Buchanan, in reply to a resolution of the House of Representatives, inquiring into the state of the defenses of Washington, from which the following extracts are made: —

"The scope of the question submitted by the House will be sufficiently met by dealing with the facts as they exist, irrespective of the cause from which they have proceeded. That revolution has been distinguished by a boldness and completeness of success rarely equalled in the history of civil commotions. Its overthrow of the Federal authority has not only been sudden and widespread, but has been marked by excesses which have alarmed all, and been sources of profound humiliation to a large portion of the American people. Its history is a history of surprises and treacheries, and ruthless spoliations. The forts of the United States have been captured and garrisoned, and hostile flags unfurled upon their ramparts. Its arsenals have been seized, and the vast amount of public arms they contained appropriated to the use of the captors; while more than half a million of dollars, found in the mint at New Orleans, have been unscrupulously applied to replenish the coffers of Louisiana. Officers in command of revenue cutters of the United States have been prevailed on to violate their trusts, and surrender the property in their charge; and instead of being branded for their crimes, they and the vessels they betrayed have been cordially received into the service of the seceded States."

After reiterating the acts of the conspirators, the information that had reached his department upon the subject, the necessity for immediate and decided action, and telling the President what steps he had taken to save the government from humiliation and disgrace, Secretary Holt closes his letter as follows: —

"Already this display of life and loyalty on the part of your administration has produced the happiest effects. Public confidence has been restored, and the feverish apprehension, which it was so mortifying to contemplate, has been banished. Whatever may have been the machinations of deluded, lawless men, the execution of their purposes has been suspended, if not altogether abandoned, in view of preparations, which announce more impressively than words, that this administration is alike able and resolved to transfer in peace to the President elect the authority that, under the Constitution, belongs to him. To those, if such there be, who desire the destruction of the republic, the presence of these troops is necessarily offensive. But those who sincerely love our institutions, cannot fail to rejoice that, by this timely precaution, they have probably escaped the deep dishonor which they must have suffered had the capital, like the forts and arsenals of the South, fallen into the hands of revolutionists, who have found this great government weak, only because, in the exhaustless beneficence of its spirit, it has refused to strike, even in its own defence, lest it should wound the aggressors."

One Breshwood, a Virginian, who was in command of the revenue-cutter McLelland, infamously surrendered his vessel to the rebels at New Orleans; and Captain Morrison surrendered the revenue cutter Cass to the rebels at Mobile. The rebels seized Fort Morgan at Mobile, and called upon Lieutenant John N. Maffit, who was in command of the Crusader, which was exposed to the fire of the fort, to surrender his vessel to the "Alabama Navy." The noble lieutenant replied, "I may be overpowered; but in that event, what will be left of the Crusader will not be worth taking." He saved his vessel, which afterwards rendered signal service in the Gulf.

On the 3d of February, 1861, Lieutenant J. H. Hamilton, of South Carolina, ordered Captain Porter to surrender his ship to the rebels. The following is Captain Porter's noble reply: "You, sir, have called upon your brother officers, not only to become traitors to their country, but to betray their sacred trust, and deliver up the ships under their command. This infamous appeal would, in ordinary times, be treated with the contempt it deserves. But I feel it a duty I owe myself, and brother officers with whom I am associated, to reply, and state, that all under my command are true and loyal to the 'Stars and Stripes,' and to the Constitution. My duty is plain before me. The constitutional government of the United States has entrusted me with the command of this beautiful ship, and before I will permit any other flag than the 'Stars and Stripes' to fly at her peak, I will fire a pistol into her magazine, and blow her up. This is my answer to your infamous letter."

For a few days before the inauguration, Washington was full of rumors of plots to prevent by violence its consummation. General Scott and Secretary Holt had been bending all their energies to gather a military force sufficient to keep in check, or suppress, if it should show itself, any lawless demonstration, and to insure peace and quiet. An imposing military escort was provided to attend the President to the Capitol, and, after the ceremonies of inauguration, to the White House.

The procession, consisting of civilians, about one thousand regulars, and a considerable force of uniformed militia, escorted the retiring and incoming

Presidents, who were in the same carriage, to the Capitol. On the spacious eastern portico of the Capitol a platform had been erected, the space in front of which was occupied by the military. The platform was occupied by the Supreme Court, members of the Senate and House of Representatives, foreign ministers, and an immense crowd of privileged persons. The President elect was introduced by Colonel Edward D. Baker, senator from Oregon, and was received with cheers from but a small share of the thirty thousand persons assembled. Mr. Lincoln, in a clear, firm, penetrating voice, delivered his inaugural address, which closed with the following paragraphs: —

"In your hands, my dissatisfied fellow-countrymen, and not in mine, is the momentous issue of civil war. The government will not assail you.

"You can have no conflict without being yourselves the aggressors. You can have no oath registered in heaven to destroy the government, while I shall have the most solemn one to 'preserve, protect, and defend it.'

"I am loath to close. We are not enemies, but friends. We must not be enemies. Though passion may have strained, it must not break our bonds of affection.

"The mystic chords of memory, stretching from every battle-field and patriot grave to every living heart and hearthstone all over this broad land, will yet swell the chorus of the Union when again touched, as surely they will be, by the better angels of our nature."

The oath of office was administered by Chief Justice Taney; the procession was re-formed, and escorted President Lincoln to the White House. Although there were many low mutterings and threats, open and implied, the arrangements were so admirably made and carried out by the loyal men at the capital, that everything connected with the ceremonies of inauguration passed off without interruption or disturbance.

The next day after his inauguration, President Lincoln submitted to the Senate the names of the gentlemen whom he had appointed as his Cabinet officers, as follows: William H. Seward, of New York, Secretary of State; Salmon P. Chase, of Ohio, Secretary of the Treasury; Simon Cameron, of Pennsylvania, Secretary of War; Gideon Welles, of Connecticut, Secretary of the Navy; Caleb B. Smith, of Indiana, Secretary of the Interior; Edward Bates, of Missouri, Attorney General; Montgomery Blair, of Maryland, Postmaster General.

The rebel capital was established at Montgomery, Alabama. Jefferson Davis had already appointed his Cabinet, as follows: Robert Toombs, of Georgia, Secretary of State; Charles G. Memminger, of South

Carolina, Secretary of the Treasury; Leroy Pope Walker, of Alabama, Secretary of War; Stephen R. Mallory, of Florida, Secretary of the Navy; John H. Reagan, of Texas, Postmaster General.

Thus were the two governments organized. President Lincoln and a majority of his Cabinet hoped that all differences between the self-styled Confederate government and the government of the United States would be adjusted without a resort to arms; while Jefferson Davis's government, which by this time had relinquished the idea of a revolution, and set themselves up as independent States, asked only to be let alone, to be allowed to possess all the property of the United States that they had stolen, and to be acknowledged as independent States. While the Confederate States claimed the right to secede from the Union, and set up a government of their own, the government of the United States denied that right, and claimed that they were still part of the Union, and subject to its Constitution and laws.

Major Robert Anderson, with a mere handful of men, — not more than eighty in all, — was placed in charge of the fortifications in Charleston harbor. They mainly tenanted Fort Moultrie, — the older and weaker of them, — being the most convenient to the city; but it could not have been held twenty-four hours against a serious assault. Its garrison was surrounded by a numerous and frowning foe. During the night of the 26th of December, 1860, Major Anderson prudently transferred his entire force to Fort Sumter, — the most impregnable of all the forts in the harbor, — taking such munitions and provisions as he could, destroying the rest, and spiking the guns, so that they could not be used by the rebels against Sumter. This was a great surprise to the rebels, and they complained of it as a breach of faith, as it was alleged that President Buchanan had promised that the military *status* should not be changed without due notice. On the 27th, — the next day after the evacuation by Major Anderson, — the rebels seized Forts Moultrie and Pickens; and about the same time the Federal arsenal at Charleston, containing many thousand stands of arms and a large quantity of military stores, was seized by the volunteers flocking to that city, by direction of the State authorities. Castle Pinckney, Fort Moultrie, and Sullivan's Island were now occupied by the rebels, and their defenses enlarged and improved, while the custom-house, post-office, and other government buildings were likewise appropriated, without resistance, the Federal officers there all being secessionists, and the palmetto flag raised over them. Iron-clad batteries had been erected in such number as to command all the entrances to Charleston harbor, so that no wooden frigate could pass them, and precluded the possibility of sending reënforcements or supplies to Fort Sumter. The Star of the West was sent from New York with reënforcements and supplies on the 5th of January, which fact was telegraphed by conspirators to their friends in Charleston. She appeared off the bar at Charleston on the 9th, and, when nearing Fort Sumter, was fired upon from Fort Moultrie and Morris's Island, and was struck by one shot. Without communicating with Major Anderson, she put about, and steered for New York. This was the last attempt made to relieve Major Anderson in his most embarrassed condition, until early in April, after the inauguration of the new government, when vessels laden with provisions were sent from New York, and arrived off the bar on the 12th, the day on which fire was opened upon Sumter. The fleet also returned to New York without fulfilling its mission, only having communicated with Major Anderson by signals.

Such was the situation of affairs on the 12th day of April, 1861, when the rebels of South Carolina opened the most wicked and causeless war upon their government ever recorded in history. In the four succeeding years events of immense magnitude and importance have transpired, affecting more or less seriously every nook and corner of our widely extended country, and carrying sadness and mourning to almost every fireside in the land.

On the 11th, General Beauregard demanded the surrender of Fort Sumter to the Confederate Government, which Major Anderson declined to do, but suggested that he would very soon be starved out, if supplies were not sent him. General Beauregard then asked of Major Anderson to state at what time he would evacuate Fort Sumter, if unmolested; and was answered that he would do so at noon on the 15th, "should I not receive, prior to that time, controlling instructions from my government, or additional supplies." This reply was not satisfactory; and, at 3.20, A. M., on the 12th, Major Anderson was notified that fire would be opened on Fort Sumter in one hour.

At the appointed moment the bombardment commenced. Fire was almost simultaneously opened from Fort Moultrie, an iron-clad floating battery in the harbor, Cummings Point, and Mount Pleasant. Fifty breaching cannon playing upon the fort, followed by the crashing and crumbling of brick, stone, and mortar, admonished Major Anderson and his small force of seventy true men, that their stay in the fort must be short, unless relieved by a more powerful fleet than our government then possessed. At seven o'clock, after breakfast,— the principal part of which was salt pork, — the command was divided into three reliefs, each in succession to man the guns for four hours. Captain Arthur Doubleday was in command of the first squad, and fired the first gun, which was directed upon Fort Moultrie. Major Anderson had determined to make the best resistance in his power, though fully aware that the fort must soon succumb to the greatly superior force with which he had to contend, while he took the greatest care that his men should be exposed as little as possible to the shot and shells of the enemy, which were falling in every direction around them.

Red-hot shot and bursting shells soon set the wooden barracks on fire, and nearly the whole interior of the fort blazed like a furnace. For thirty-six hours the terrific bombardment continued, with but occasional lulls. The garrison in Sumter soon became so exhausted that they could make but a feeble response. The scene inside the fort is described by an eye-witness, as follows: —

"The fire surrounded us on all sides. Fearful that the walls might crack, and the shells pierce and prostrate them, we commenced taking the powder out of the magazine before the fire had fully enveloped it. We took ninety-six barrels of powder out, and threw them into the sea, leaving two hundred barrels in it. Owing to a lack of cartridges, we kept five men inside the magazine, serving as we wanted them, thus using up our shirts, sheets, blankets, and all the available material in the fort. When we were finally obliged to close the magazine, and our material for cartridges was exhausted, we were left destitute of any means to continue the contest. We had eaten our last biscuit thirty-six hours before. We came very near being stifled with the dense, livid smoke from the burning buildings. Many of the men lay prostrate on the ground, with wet handkerchiefs over their mouths and eyes, gasping for breath. It was a moment of imminent peril. If an eddy of wind had not ensued, we all probably should have been suffocated. The crashing of the shot, the bursting of the shells, the falling of the walls, and the roar of the flames, made a Pandemonium of the fort. We, nevertheless, kept up a steady fire."

On the afternoon of the second day of the bombardment, Louis T. Wigfall, late a United States senator from Texas, made his appearance in a small boat, with a white flag, and was admitted; and in a conference with Major Anderson and his officers, insisted that further resistance was useless. The fort was on fire, the garrison exhausted, with the Stars and Stripes floating defiantly over the ruins. Another deputation soon arrived, Wigfall having failed to agree with Major Anderson on the terms for a surrender. After some conference, it was agreed that the garrison should surrender the fort, taking with them, as they retired at their leisure, and in their own way, all their individual and company property, their side arms, and their tattered flag, which they were to salute with a hundred guns, before they hauled it down.

The battle ceased; the fire was extinguished, after destroying almost everything combustible in the fort. Next morning, about nine o'clock, the evacuation took place, while the guns of the fort boomed a salute to the lowering flag, which had been so bravely defended against the unequal foe. The garrison marched out of the main gate, preceded by the band playing "Yankee Doodle" and "Hail Columbia," with the Stars and Stripes floating over them. They embarked on board the United States ship Baltic, and were carried to New York, where they met with an enthusiastic reception.

That seven thousand well drilled men, with all the needed appliances, could overcome seventy, out of provisions, — for they had eaten their last biscuit, — and nearly destitute of ammunition, and with no hope of succor, was regarded by the chivalry of South Carolina as a most wonderful and glorious victory, and as establishing beyond dispute the independence of the Confederacy.

Arrived at New York, Major Anderson despatched to his government the following report: —

"STEAMSHIP BALTIC, OFF SANDY HOOK,
April 18, 1861,
"THE HON. S. CAMERON,
" *Secretary of War, Washington, D. C.*

"Sir: Having defended Fort Sumter for thirty-four hours, until the quarters were entirely burned, the main gates destroyed, the gorge wall seriously injured, the magazine surrounded by flames, ánd its door closed from the effects of the heat, four barrels and three cartridges of powder only being available, and no provisions but pork remaining, I accepted terms of evacuation offered by General Beauregard (being the same offered by him on the 11th instant, prior to the commencement of hostilities), and marched out of the fort on Sunday afternoon, the 14th instant, with colors flying and drums beating, bringing away company and private property, and saluting my flag with fifty guns.

"ROBERT ANDERSON,
"*Major First Artillery.*"

On the next day after the evacuation of Fort Sumter, April 15, President Lincoln issued a call for seventy-five thousand volunteers for three months' service, and called an extra session of Congress to meet on the ensuing 4th of July. The uprising of the freemen of the North was such as the world never witnessed before. The insult to the old honored flag created a feeling of the most intense indignation, and all party lines seemed for the time obliterated, and two parties only had an existence, — those who would destroy the Union, on the one hand, and those who would defend and preserve it, at any cost, on the other.

There were many who believed that the state of feeling which had resulted in an open rebellion of the slaveholders against the government, had been produced by extremists both at the North and the South, instead of attributing the difficulty to its true cause,— the wide difference between a society of educated freemen and a society of slaveholders and slaves, where only the few were educated; but there were none in the free States who openly justified the assault upon Fort Sumter.

On the 15th of April the President promulgated the following

"Proclamation.

"Whereas, the laws of the United States have been for some time past, and now are, opposed, and the execution thereof obstructed, in the States of South Carolina, Georgia, Alabama, Florida, Mississippi, Louisiana, and Texas, by combinations, too powerful to be suppressed by the ordinary course of judicial proceedings, or by the powers vested in the marshals by law: Now, therefore, I, Abraham Lincoln, President of the United States, in virtue of the power in me vested by the Constitution and the laws, have thought fit to call forth the militia of the several States of the Union, to the aggregate number of seventy-five thousand, in order to suppress said combinations, and to cause the laws to be duly executed.

"The details of this object will be immediately communicated to the State authorities, through the War Department. I appeal to all loyal citizens to favor, facilitate, and aid this effort to maintain the honor, the integrity, and existence of our national Union, and the perpetuity of popular government, and to redress wrongs already long enough endured. I deem it proper to say, that the first service assigned to the forces hereby called forth, will probably be to repossess the forts, places, and property which have been seized from the Union. And, in every event, the utmost care will be observed, consistently with the objects aforesaid, to avoid any devastation, any destruction of, or interference with, property, or any disturbance of peaceful citizens of any part of the country. And I hereby command the persons comprising the combinations aforesaid to disperse, and retire peaceably to their respective abodes, within twenty days from this date.

"Deeming that the present condition of public affairs presents an extraordinary occasion, I do hereby, by virtue of the power in me vested by the Constitution, convene both Houses of Congress. The Senators and Representatives are, therefore, summoned to assemble at their respective chambers, at twelve o'clock, noon, on Thursday, the fourth day of July next, then and there to consider and determine such measures as, in their wisdom, the public safety and interest may seem to demand.

"In witness whereof, I have hereunto set my hand, and caused the seal of the United States to be affixed.

"Done at the city of Washington, the fifteenth day of April, in the year of our Lord one thousand eight hundred and sixty-one, and of the independence of the United States the eighty-fifth.

"ABRAHAM LINCOLN.
"By the President:
"WILLIAM H. SEWARD, *Secretary of State.*"

With this proclamation, was sent from the War Department, to the Governors of the several States, a circular, explaining that the call was for regiments of infantry, or riflemen only, each regiment to be composed of seven hundred and eighty men. They were apportioned to the several States as follows: Maine,

New Hampshire, Vermont, Rhode Island, Connecticut, Delaware, Arkansas, Michigan, Iowa, Minnesota, and Wisconsin, one each; Massachusetts, Tennessee, and North Carolina, two each; New Jersey, Maryland, and Kentucky, four each; Indiana and Illinois, six each; New York, seventeen; Pennsylvania, sixteen; and Ohio, thirteen. These ninety-four regiments would make a total of seventy-three thousand three hundred and twenty men. The residue of the seventy-five thousand was to be furnished by the District of Columbia.

The Governors of the States of Virginia, North Carolina, Tennessee, and Kentucky utterly refused to furnish any men for the purpose named in the proclamation. The response of Governor Harris, of Tennessee, was as follows, and may be taken as a fair sample of the replies from the Governors of all the above-named States:—

"Tennessee will not furnish a single man for coercion; but fifty thousand, if necessary for the defense of our rights, and *those of our brethren.*"

Governor Jackson, of Missouri, in reply to the call, said,—

"It is illegal, unconstitutional, revolutionary, inhuman, diabolical, and cannot be complied with. Not one man will the State of Missouri furnish to carry on so unholy a crusade."

Governor Burton, of Delaware, took until the 26th of April to consider the matter, and then replied, that "The laws of this State do not confer upon the Executive any authority allowing him to comply with such requisition."

Governor Hicks, of Maryland, though claiming to be a Unionist himself, and that his State was still in the Union, gave the Union cause but a very cold support when called upon for troops to uphold it. On the 18th of April he issued a proclamation to the people of Maryland, assuring them that he should do all in his power to preserve "the honor and integrity of the State, and to maintain within her limits that peace so earnestly desired by all good citizens." And adding, "No troops will be sent from Maryland, unless it may be for the defense of the national capital."

On the 17th of April, Jefferson Davis, the head of a band of conspirators and rebels, issued a proclamation, authorizing privateers to be fitted out from all parts of the South, to prey upon the commerce of the United States, and this, too, when the North had been robbed by these conspirators of its entire naval force, and had not half a dozen vessels which could be called into our waters to protect our merchant marine.

As a protection against this piratical proclamation, President Lincoln, on the 19th of April, announced the blockade of all the ports of the seceded States.

As if by magic a naval force sprang into existence, and in less than ninety days over three hundred armed vessels of war were sailing beneath the Stars and Stripes, with brave men upon their decks, ready to avenge any insult to their honored flag.

About this time there was a determination on the part of leading rebels to capture the City of Washington at all hazards. The Richmond Examiner, of April 23d, said, "The capture of Washington City is perfectly within the power of Virginia and Maryland, if Virginia will only make the effort by her constituted authorities. The entire population pant for the onset. Our people can take it; they will take it; and Scott, the arch-traitor, and Lincoln, the beast, combined, cannot prevent it."

It has been conclusively proved that the following was the plot for the capture of the capital of the nation, with all the public property. A conspiracy was formed by leading Virginians, with prominent secessionists in Washington, and a band of traitors of influence and wealth in Baltimore, to accomplish the infamous and cowardly act in the following manner: Virginia did not then pretend to be out of the Union, and was fully represented in both branches of Congress. The Virginians, at the head of between two and three thousand desperate men, were to make a descent upon Harper's Ferry, seize the arsenal there, which contained twenty-five thousand stand of arms, and thus supply themselves with an abundance of weapons and ammunition. They were then to descend the Potomac to Washington, and make a fierce onset in the streets of the city. Traitors there, in strong bands, armed to the teeth, were prepared to receive them. Incendiaries were designated to fire the city at several points. Amid the terror and confusion of this sudden assault, the conspirators were to seize the most important government buildings, and convert them into fortresses, where they could defy any immediate attack from the bewildered government, and whence they could command the city.

While all this was being done, the conspirators in Baltimore were to cut off all communication with the North, by burning bridges, tearing up railways, and seizing the post-office and telegraph stations. Should troops attempt to reach Washington from the North, a mob was to destroy them in the streets of Baltimore. Troops were to rush from the South to the captured city, and occupy all important military stations. Virginia and Maryland were thus to be dragged into secession, and Washington was to be the capital of the Southern Confederacy.

When this damnable plot was discovered, just on the eve of its execution, it seemed almost impossible for the government to thwart it. Washington was filled with traitors and rebels; no reliance could be placed upon the militia; Southern traitors were occupying the most important posts in the army, and the government did not know who could be trusted. The government seemed surrounded with difficulties, from which there seemed to be no way of extrication; and the North, though burning to avenge the insult upon the flag in the unprovoked attack upon Sumter, had not begun to comprehend the extent of the danger to the national capital, and it is doubtful if they do now, or ever will, since the government passed the crisis more easily than the most sanguine had reason to hope it would.

This plot was made known on the 18th of April, confidentially, to the loyal people of Washington, and gentlemen temporarily there, who were known to be friends of the Union. A gentleman who was there, and took part in the transactions, says, —

"A few trusty friends of the government, visitors in Washington, immediately commenced vigorous, but secret measures, to assist the administration in this fearful crisis. They hastened, by committees, to all the hotels, and sought out those known to be true to the Union, informed them of the peril, and appointed a meeting that very evening, in the church in the rear of Willard's Hotel, where they would not attract attention. Solemnly, and with intense emotion, they administered the oath anew, of fidelity to the national flag, to every one to whom they confided the secret, and then gave to each the pass which would admit him to the church. This work was speedily accomplished, for there was not a moment to be lost, and soon about two hundred men were assembled in the church.

"After listening to a few words of eloquence, which yet burn in the souls of some of the volunteers in that dark night of the nation's peril, the company formed themselves into the noted 'CASSIUS M. CLAY BATTALION.' These noble men, many of whom were among the most distinguished for wealth and position to be found in our land, were enrolled under efficient officers into small patrol parties, and marched all night long through the streets of the city, to guard against incendiaries, and to prevent the assembling of conspirators. They had orders to shoot down promptly any who should resist their authority."

Another party of three hundred men were also appointed, under General Lane, to go unobserved to the White House, and bivouac in the East Room, ready to give a warm reception to any parties who might make a sudden attack upon the Presidential Mansion. For three weeks the East Room was thus occupied. General Scott promptly took unobserved possession of the Capitol, with a sufficient number of men to maintain a desperate defense, where were deposited great quantities of military stores and provisions. Thus was the White House and the Capitol to be held until troops from the North could fight their way through Maryland for their rescue if besieged. The greatest care was exercised by the government to guard against surprise.

At ten o'clock, on the night of the 19th, Lieutenant Jones, of the United States army, who was in command at Harper's Ferry, with but forty-three men, received reliable information that Governor Letcher, of Virginia, had sent three thousand State troops, via Winchester, and that they would reach Harper's Ferry in two hours; and that three hundred troops, from Hallstown, were within twenty minutes' march of the arsenal. Combustibles had been previously prepared, and everything in readiness to blow up the arsenal and other buildings of the armory, should he find the enemy coming upon him in overwhelming numbers. In a trice the torch was applied, and the buildings were all in a blaze, and Lieutenant Jones, with his forty-three men, retreated across the bridge into Maryland, and, after marching all night, reached Carlisle, Pennsylvania, where they were safe from attack from the traitors. The secessionists at the Ferry rushed to the arsenal, and vainly attempted to extinguish the flames. In their rage, they pursued the heroic band, and, firing upon them, killed two of their number. Before morning nearly five thousand Virginia troops were in possession of the ruins at Harper's Ferry.

On the 17th of April, a convention in Virginia secretly passed an ordinance of secession, which was for a time kept from the knowledge of the community, that more effectual measures might be adopted for seizing the government property and fortifications in that State, though a private messenger was sent to inform the Confederate government of the action of the convention.

Government property, to the amount of many millions of dollars, was accumulated at Norfolk Navy Yard, including machine-shops, founderies, storehouses, together with immense amounts of naval and military stores, the whole estimated as worth over nine millions of dollars. The new steam-frigate Merrimac, the Pennsylvania, the largest line-of-battle ship in the world, the Germantown, the Dolphin, and other war vessels, were floating in the harbor. By order of Governor Letcher, on the night of the 16th of April, a large number of boats, laden with stone, were sunk in the channel, so that these large vessels could not pass out, and arrangements were made for seizing the yard. Captain McCaulay was in command of the yard, and most of the sub-officers were traitors.

It became evident that the yard could not be held, but that it must fall into the hands of the rebels, and it was determined to destroy it; and the steamship Pawnee was sent from Fortress Monroe to aid in the work. When she appeared at Norfolk, she met with a most enthusiastic welcome from the crews of the Pennsylvania, and other war vessels lying there. The Pawnee arrived, and made fast to the dock at Norfolk about nine o'clock on the evening of the 21st of April, immediately landed her troops, and seized the gates of the yard, so that no traitors could enter. Everything of value was removed from the Pennsylvania. What could not be removed was thrown overboard, and every preparation made for a great conflagration. At four o'clock next morning, all the men from the yard, except a few left to fire the trains, which had been carefully laid, were taken on board the Cumberland and Pawnee, and the former took the latter vessel in tow. At a given signal the torch was applied, and everything combustible, including the Pennsylvania and several other war vessels, was destroyed.

To put down this well-planned and most wicked rebellion, the North, as one man, nobly responded to the call of President Lincoln for troops. On the evening of the eighteenth, four hundred Pennsylvania volunteers reached Washington. On the same day the Sixth Regiment of Massachusetts volunteers left Boston for Washington, and arrived at Baltimore on the 19th, where they were joined by a regiment from Philadelphia. The Philadelphia regiment was without arms, and the Sixth Massachusetts was but partially armed.

In passing from one railroad station to another in Baltimore, a distance of two and a half miles, the cars had to be drawn by horses. The Massachusetts and Philadelphia troops occupied seventeen cars. The five foremost cars, containing a portion of the Massachusetts troops, were sent forward. There being no horses for the other cars, the residue of the regiment, of whom but a small portion were armed, left the cars and formed in the street, waiting the arrival of horses. None came, for a secession mob which filled the streets had covered the track, immediately behind the cars which had been sent forward, with heavy timbers, anchors, stones, and other obstructions, to prevent the passage of the other cars. The residue of the regiment were assailed by the mob with showers of stones and other missiles, hurled from the streets and house-tops, and several soldiers were knocked down and badly injured. In the confusion, one of the rioters stepped up behind a young soldier, seized his gun, and shot him dead. At this the soldiers were ordered to fire, and those who had loaded muskets obeyed the order, with some effect, which caused the mob to recoil. The soldiers, learning that the track had been obstructed, commenced their march from the Camden to the Washington depot, surrounded and followed by the mob, preceded by Mayor Brown and a strong detachment of police. The mob closed in, and attempted to cut off a portion of the rear, which being hardly pressed was ordered to fire, which they did. Several volleys were fired by a small portion of the regiment, killing eleven and wounding four of the rioters. Three soldiers were killed and eight seriously injured. The Massachusetts regiment finally reached the Washington depot, and were sent forward to Washington. The train was repeatedly fired at from the hills and woods along the route, but no one was injured. The Philadelphia regiment having no arms, after a hand-to-hand fight with the mob, returned to that city.

The telegraph wires connecting Baltimore and the free States were cut, and the railroad bridges northward and north-westward from Baltimore, on the railroads to Philadelphia and Harrisburg, were burned, thus shutting off Washington from all communication with the Northern States. In the mean time, however, the North was making all possible haste in enlisting, arming, equipping, and making ready for the field her noble and patriotic sons.

ACTION OF VERMONT.

THE breaking out of the slaveholders' rebellion, found the militia of Vermont, as in most of the other Northern States, in a disorganized and inefficient condition. The enrollment required by law was imperfect, many towns having neglected to make returns, and there were no records from which the number of men required by statute to perform military duty in case of insurrection or invasion could be ascertained with any degree of accuracy. In the adjutant-general's office were the names of twenty-two organized uniformed companies, all of which were deficient in numbers, and some were without arms.

Such was the state of things on the 15th of April, when President Lincoln called for seventy-five thousand volunteers for three months, to suppress an insurrection against the government of the United States, which had broken out in the States of South Carolina, Georgia, Alabama, Florida, Mississippi,

VERMONT STATE HOUSE.

Louisiana, and Texas. On that day Governor Erastus Fairbanks received a copy of the call for troops, — the quota of Vermont being one regiment, — and immediately issued the proper orders to H. H. Baxter, of Rutland, Adjutant and Inspector General, and called an extra session of the Legislature, to commence on the 23d of the same month, to adopt measures for the State to do promptly its share toward meeting the exigencies of the country, by organizing, uniforming, arming, and equipping the militia within her borders.

The members of the Legislature responded with alacrity to the call of the Governor. They enacted a law, giving to each member of a uniformed military company who should be called into the service of the United States, under the requisition of the President, seven dollars per month in addition to the pay allowed by the United States government, which was afterwards construed so as to include all troops from the State; — and that each member of a uniformed company, held in readiness for active service, should be paid eighteen dollars per month by the State of Vermont. They also enacted another law for the relief of families of volunteers; and another, making an appropriation of one million dollars for the purpose of more perfectly organizing, arming, equipping, drilling, and providing for the militia of the State, and for other purposes connected with the suppression of the rebellion. Also another "act to provide for raising six special regiments for immediate service, for defending and protecting the Constitution and the Union."

George J. Stannard of St. Albans, then Colonel of the Fourth regiment, Vermont militia, and second ranking colonel in the State, was the first man who offered his services to put down the rebellion. Immediately on the assault upon Fort Sumter, he corresponded with commanders of companies in his regiment, and having obtained their approval, tendered his services, with his regiment, in any place that they might be required to defend the flag. The tender was made by telegraph to Governor Fairbanks, and also to General Jackman, who was commander of all the Vermont militia. The regiment was formally accepted, but it was subsequently decided that the first regiment called for should be made up from all the volunteer militia of the State, and the Adjutant General selected the companies to compose it, as follows:—

First Regiment.

Colonel, J. Wolcott Phelps of Brattleboro'; Lieut.-Colonel, Peter T. Washburn of Woodstock; Major, Harry N. Worthen of Bradford.

Co. A, Green Mountain Guards, Swanton. Captain, Lawrence D. Clark; First Lieut., Albert B. Jewett; Second Lieut., John D. Sheriden.

Co. B, Woodstock Light Infantry, Woodstock. Captain, William W Pelton; First Lieut., Andrew J. Dike; Second Lieut., Solomon E. Woodward.

Co. C, Ransom Guards, St. Albans. Captain, Charles G. Chandler; First Lieut., Hiram E. Perkins; Second Lieut., Freeborn E. Bell.

Co. D, Bradford Guards, Bradford. Captain, Dudley K. Andros; First Lieut., John B. Pickett; Second Lieut., Roswell Farnham.

Co. E, Cavendish Light Infantry, Cavendish. Captain, Oscar S. Tuttle; First Lieut., Asaph Clark; Second Lieut., Salmon Dutton.

Co. F, New England Guards, Northfield. Captain, William H. Boynton; First Lieut., Charles C. Webb; Second Lieut., Francis B. Gove.

Co. G, Allen Guards, Brandon. Captain, Joseph Bush; First Lieut., William Cronan; Second Lieut., Ebenezer J. Ormsbee.

Co. H, Howard Guards, Burlington. Captain, David B. Peck; First Lieut., Oscar G. Mower; Second Lieut., George J. Hagar.

Co. I, Union Guards, Middlebury. Captain, Eben S. Hayward; First Lieut., Charles W Rose; Second Lieut., Orville W Heath.

Co. K, Rutland Light Infantry, Rutland. Captain, William Y. W Ripley; First Lieut., George T. Roberts; Second Lieut., Levi G. Kingsley.

The companies rendezvoused at Rutland on the 2d of May, were mustered into the United States service on the 9th, and left the State for the seat of war on the same day. The regiment arrived at Fortress Monroe on the 13th, and on the 27th removed to Newport News, Va., where it remained until the 5th of August. On the 10th of June, companies B, D, F, H, and K, under command of Lieut.-Col. Washburn, were engaged in the battle of Big Bethel, and did good service. On the arrival of the regiment at Newport News, Colonel Phelps was made commander of the post, and remained there after the regiment returned home, and was subsequently appointed Brigadier General. On the 5th of August, the regiment, under command of Lieut.-Colonel Washburn, left Newport News for Brattleboro', where it went into camp, and was mustered out of service on the 15th. Most of the officers and men of this regiment afterwards entered other organizations, and served with distinction during the war.

On the 3d of May, the President called for twenty thousand volunteers for three years. Under this call, orders were issued for raising by enlistment, the Second and Third Regiments, to serve for three years or during the war.

SECOND REGIMENT.

The following were the field and line officers, the companies and their locations, which composed this regiment: —

Colonel Henry Whiting; Lieut. Colonel, George J. Stannard; Major, Charles H. Joyce.

Co. A, Bennington. Captain, James H. Walbridge; First Lieut., Newton Stone; Second Lieut., William H. Cady.

Co. B, Castleton. Captain, James Hope; First Lieut., John Howe; Second Lieut., Enoch Johnson.

Co. C, Brattleboro' Captain, Edward A. Todd; First Lieut., John S. Tyler; Second Lieut., Henry C. Campbell.

Co. D, Waterbury. Captain, Charles Dillingham; First Lieut., William W Henry; Second Lieut., Charles C. Gregg.

Co. E, Tunbridge. Captain, Richard Smith; First Lieut., Lucius C. Whitney; Second Lieut., Orville Bixby.

Co. F, Montpelier. Captain, Francis V Randall; First Lieut., Walter A. Phillips; Second Lieut., Horace F. Crossman.

Co. G, Burlington. Captain, John T. Drew; First

Lieut., David L. Sharpley; Second Lieut., Anson H. Weed.

Co. H., Fletcher. Captain, William T. Burnham; First Lieut., Jerome B. Case; Second Lieut., Charles K. Leach.

Co. I., Ludlow, Captain, Volney S. Fullam; First Lieut., Sherman W Parkhurst; Second Lieut., Isaac N. Wadleigh.

Co. K., Vergennes. Captain, Solon Eaton; First Lieut., Amasa S. Tracy; Second Lieut., Jonathan M. Hoyt.

This regiment rendezvoused at Burlington, was mustered into the United States service on the 20th of June, 1861, and consisted of eight hundred and sixty-eight officers and men. It left the State for the seat of war on the 24th of June, and was engaged in the first battle of Bull Run on the 21st of July, 1861. This, together with the Third, Fourth, Fifth, and Sixth Regiments, constituted the "Vermont Brigade," a more particular account of the operations of which is given in another place.

Third Regiment.

The following were the field and line officers, the companies and their locations, which composed this regiment:—

Colonel, William F. Smith; Lieut. Colonel, Breed N. Hyde; Major, Walter W Cochran.

Co. A, Springfield. Captain, Wheelock G. Veazey; First Lieut., Frederick Crain; Second Lieut., Horace W Floyd.

Co. B, Coventry. Captain, Augustine C. West; First Lieut., Enoch H. Bartlett; Second Lieut., John H. Coburn.

Co. C, Wells River. Captain, David T. Corbin; First Lieut., Danford C. Haviland; Second Lieut., Edwin M. Noyes.

Co. D, Charleston. Captain, Fernando C. Harrington; First Lieut., Daniel J. Kenneson; Second Lieut., Charles Bishop.

Co. E, Johnson. Captain, Andrew J. Blanchard; First Lieut., Robert D. Whittemore; Second Lieut., Burr J. Austin.

Co. F, Hartford. Captain, Thomas O. Seaver; First Lieut., Samuel E. Pingree; Second Lieut., Edward A. Chandler.

Co. G, St. Johnsbury. Captain, Lorenzo D. Allen; First Lieut., John H. Hutchinson; Second Lieut., Moses F. Brown.

Co. H, St. Albans. Captain, Thomas F. House; First Lieut., Waterman F. Corey; Second Lieut., Romeo H. Start.

Co. I, Guildhall. Captain, Thomas Nelson; First

Lieut., James Powers; Second Lieut., Alexander W. Beattie.

Co. K, Calais. Captain, Elon O. Hammond; First Lieut., Amasa T. Smith; Second Lieut., Alonzo E. Pierce.

This regiment rendezvoused at St. Johnsbury, was mustered into the United States service on the 15th of July, 1861, and consisted of eight hundred and eighty-two officers and men. It left the State for the seat of war on the 26th of July, and formed a part of the "Vermont Brigade."

FOURTH REGIMENT.

The field and line officers of the Fourth Regiment were as follows: —

Colonel, Edwin H. Stoughton; Lieut. Colonel, Harry N. Worthen; Major, John C. Tyler.

Co. A. Captain, John E. Pratt; First Lieut., Albert K. Parsons; Second Lieut., Gideon H. Benton.

Co. B. Captain, James H. Platt, Jr.; First Lieut., Albert K. Nichols; Second Lieut., Samuel H. Chamberlin.

Co. C. Captain, Henry B. Atherton; First Lieut., George B. French; Second Lieut., Daniel D. Wheeler.

Co. D. Captain, George Tucker; First Lieut., Geo. W Quimby; Second Lieut., John H. Bishop.

Co. E. Captain, Henry L. Terry; First Lieut., Stephen M. Pingree; Second Lieut., Daniel Lillie.

Co. F. Captain, Addison Brown, Jr.; First Lieut., William C. Holbrook; Second Lieut., Daniel W Farr.

Co. G. Captain, George P. Foster; First Lieut., Henry H. Hill; Second Lieut., Joseph W D. Carpenter.

Co. H. Captain, Robert W. Laird; First Lieut., Albert W Fisher; Second Lieut., J. Byron Brooks.

Co. I. Captain, Leonard A. Stearns; First Lieut., Levi M. Tucker; Second Lieut., Albert A. Allard.

Co. K. Captain, Frank B. Gove; First Lieut., Charles W Boutin; Second Lieut., William C. Tracy.

The Fourth Regiment rendezvoused at Brattleboro', was mustered into the United States service on the 21st of September, 1861, numbering ten hundred and forty-two men, and left the State for the seat of war the same day. This regiment was also joined to the "Vermont Brigade."

Fifth Regiment.

The following were the field and line officers, and the companies and their locations, which formed the Fifth Regiment: —

Colonel, Henry A. Smalley; Lieut. Colonel, Nathan Lord, Jr.; Major, Lewis A. Grant.

Co. A, St. Albans. Captain, Charles G. Chandler; First Lieut., Alonzo R. Hurlburt; Second Lieut., Lucius M. D. Smith.

Co. B, Middlebury. Captain, Charles W Rose; First Lieut., Wilson D. Wright; Second Lieut., Olney A. Comstock.

Co. C, Swanton. Captain, John D. Sheridan; First Lieut., Friend H. Barney; Second Lieut., Jesse A. Jewett.

Co. D, Hydepark. Captain, Reuben C. Benton; First Lieut., James W Stiles; Second Lieut., Samuel Sumner, Jr.

Co. E, Manchester. Captain, Charles P Dudley; First Lieut., William H. H. Peck; Second Lieut., Samuel E. Burnham.

Co. F, Cornwall. Captain, Edwin S. Stowell; First Lieut., Cyrus R. Crane; Second Lieut., Eugene A. Hamilton.

Co. G, Rutland. Captain, Benjamin R. Jenne; First Lieut., Charles T. Allchinn; Second Lieut., Martin J. McManus.

Co. H, Brandon. Captain, Charles W. Seagar; First Lieut., Cornelius H. Forbes; Second Lieut., Charles J. Ormsbee.

Co. I, Burlington. Captain, John R. Lewis; First Lieut., William P. Spalding; Second Lieut., Henry Ballard.

Co. K, Richmond. Captain, Frederick F. Gleason; First Lieut., William Symons; Second Lieut., George J. Hatch.

GREAT REBELLION. 67

This regiment rendezvoused at St. Albans, was mustered into the United States service on the 16th of September, 1861, left the State for the seat of war on the same day, and consisted of ten hundred and six officers and men. It also formed a part of the "Vermont Brigade."

SIXTH REGIMENT.

The following were the field and line officers, and the companies constituting the Sixth Regiment: —

Colonel, Nathaniel Lord, Jr.; Lieut. Colonel, Asa P. Blunt; Major, Oscar S. Tuttle.

Co. A. Captain, George Parker, Jr.; First Lieut., Riley O. Bird; Second Lieut., Frank G. Butterfield.

Co. B. Captain, Alonzo B. Hutchinson; First Lieut., La Marquis Tubbs; Second Lieut., Bernard D. Fabyan.

Co. C. Captain, Jesse C. Spaulding; First Lieut., George C. Randall; Second Lieut., Hiram A. Kimball.

Co. D. Captain, Oscar A. Hale; First Lieut., George H. Phelps; Second Lieut., Carlos W Dwinnell.

Co. E. Captain, Edward W Barker; First Lieut., Thomas R. Clark; Second Lieut., Frank B. Bradbury.

Co. F. Captain, Edwin F. Reynolds; First Lieut., Elijah Whitney; Second Lieut., Denison A. Raxford.

Co. G. Captain, William H. H. Hall; First Lieut., Alfred M. Nevins; Second Lieut., Edwin C. Lewis.

Co. H. Captain, David B. Davenport; First Lieut., Robinson Templeton; Second Lieut., Luther Ainsworth.

Co. I. Captain, Wesley Hazelton; First Lieut., William B. Reynolds; Second Lieut., Edwin R. Kinney.

Co. K. Captain, Elisha L. Barney; First Lieut., Lucius Green; Second Lieut., Alfred H. Keith.

The Sixth Regiment rendezvoused at Montpelier, was mustered into the United States service on the 15th of October, 1861, left for the seat of war on the 20th of the same month, consisted of nine hundred and seventy-one officers and men, and formed a part of the "Vermont Brigade."

Seventh Regiment.

The following were the field and line officers, and the companies, and their locations, which composed the Seventh Regiment: —

Colonel, George T. Roberts; Lieut. Colonel, Volney S. Fullam; Major, William C. Holbrook.

Co. A, Burlington. Captain, David B. Peck; First Lieut., Heman Austin; Second Lieut., Hiram B. Fish.

Co. B, Brandon. Captain, William Cronan; First Lieut., Darwin A. Smalley; Second Lieut., Jackson V Parker.

Co. C, Middlebury. Captain, Henry M. Porter; First Lieut., Erwin V N. Hitchcock; Second Lieut., John G. Dickinson.

Co. D, Rutland. Captain, John B. Kilburn; First Lieut., William B. Thrall; Second Lieut., George E. Cross.

Co. E, Johnson. Captain, Daniel Landon; First Lieut., George W Sheldon; Second Lieut., Richard T. Cull.

Co. F, Swanton. Captain, Lorenzo D. Brooks; First Lieut., Edgar N. Ballard; Second Lieut., Rodney C. Gates.

Co. G, Cavendish. Captain, Salmon Dutton; First Lieut., George M. R. Howard; Second Lieut., Leonard P. Bingham.

Co. H, Woodstock. Captain, Mahlon M. Young; First Lieut., Henry H. French; Second Lieut., George H. Kelley.

Co. I, Poultney. Captain, Charles C. Ruggles; First Lieut., Charles Clark; Second Lieut., Austin E. Woodman.

Co. K, Northfield. Captain, Nathan P Barber; First Lieut., John L. Moseley; Second Lieut., Allen Spalding.

This regiment rendezvoused at Rutland, was mustered into the United States service on the 12th of February, 1862, consisted of ten hundred and fourteen officers and men, and left the State for the seat of war on the 10th of March.

Eighth Regiment.

The field and line officers, and the companies composing this regiment, with their locations, were as follows: —

Colonel, Stephen Thomas; Lieut. Colonel, Edward M. Brown; Major, Charles Dillingham.

Co. A, Hydepark. Captain, Luman A. Grout; First Lieut., Moses McFarland; Second Lieut., Gilman S. Rand.

Co. B, Derby Line. Captain, Charles B. Child; First Lieut., Stephen T. Spalding; Second Lieut., Frederick D. Butterfield.

Co. C, St. Johnsbury. Captain, Henry E. Foster; First Lieut., Edward B. Wright; Second Lieut., Frederick J. Fuller.

Co. D, Bradford. Captain, Cyrus B. Leach; First Lieut., Alfred E. Getchell; Second Lieut., Darius C. Child.

Co. E, Worcester. Captain, Edward Hall; First Lieut., Kilburn Day; Second Lieut., Truman Kellogg.

Co. F, St. Albans. Captain, Hiram E. Perkins; First Lieut., Daniel S. Foster; Second Lieut., Carter H. Nason.

Co. G, West Randolph. Captain, Samuel G. P Craig; First Lieut., Job W Green; Second Lieut., John B. Mead.

Co. H, Townshend. Captain, Henry F. Dutton; First Lieut., Alvin B. Franklin; Second Lieut., William H. H. Holton.

Co. I, Marlboro'. Captain, William W. Lynde; First Lieut., George N. Holland; Second Lieut., Joshua C. Morse.

Co. K, Lunenburg. Captain, John S. Clarke; First Lieut., Adoniram J. Howard; Second Lieut., George F. French.

The Eighth Regiment was raised under a special Act of the Legislature, for General Benjamin F. Butler's expedition. It rendezvoused at Brattleboro', was mustered into the United States servive on the 18th of February, 1862; consisted of ten hundred and fifteen officers and men, and left the State to join the expedition on the 6th of the following March.

FIRST VERMONT BATTERY.

The officers of this organization were, Captain, George W Duncan; Senior First Lieut., George T. Hebard; Junior First Lieut., Edward Rice; Senior Second Lieut., Henry N. Colburn; Junior Second Lieut., Salmon B. Hebard. This battery rendezvoused at Brattleboro', consisted of one hundred and fifty-six officers and men, and was attached to the Eighth Regiment. It was mustered into the United States service, and left the State to join General Butler's expedition at the same time as that regiment.

Second Vermont Battery.

The Second Vermont Battery rendezvoused at Brandon, was mustered into the United States service on the 24th of December, 1861, and consisted of one hundred and nine officers and men, commanded by Captain Lensie R. Sayles. On the next day after its muster, the battery went into camp at Lowell, Mass., and the following February left that place, and was stationed at Ship Island, New Orleans, and other places, where it performed good service.

Sharpshooters.

Early in August, 1861, Edmund Weston, Jr., of West Randolph, was authorized to raise a company of Sharpshooters for Colonel Berdan's regiment, and went vigorously about the work. The company rendezvoused at West Randolph, and consisted of one hundred and twenty-five men. The officers were, Captain, Edmund Weston, Jr.; First Lieut., Charles W Seaton; Second Lieut., Martin V. Brown. The company left for Washington on the 4th of September, and was mustered into the United States service on the 31st of October, 1861. It was attached to the First Regiment Berdan's Sharpshooters as Co. F.

The Second Company of Sharpshooters rendezvoused at West Randolph on the 1st of November, 1861, and was mustered into the United States service on the 9th, with ninety-one officers and men. The officers were, Captain, Homer R. Stoughton; First Lieut., Frederick Spaulding; Second Lieut., Henry M. Hall. It was attached to the Second Regiment Berdan's Sharpshooters as Co. E.

The Third Company of Sharpshooters was recruited at Brattleboro.' The officers were, Captain, Gilbert Hart; First Lieut., Henry Herbert; Second Lieut., Albert Baxter. It was mustered into the United States service on the 31st of December, 1861, with ninety-four officers and men. Early in February following twelve recruits were sent forward to this company, which had been attached as Co. H to the Second Regiment Berdan's Sharpshooters.

Captain William Y W Ripley, of Rutland, was appointed Lieut. Colonel of the First Regiment Sharpshooters, and commissioned by the Governor of Vermont.

FIRST REGIMENT OF CAVALRY.

In October, 1861, Samuel B. Platt was authorized by the War Department to recruit and put into the field a full regiment of cavalry from the State of Vermont. The following were the locations of the companies and the names of their officers: —

Co. A, Chittenden County. Captain, Frank A. Platt; First Lieut., Joel B. Erhardt; Second Lieut., Ellis B. Edwards.

Co. B, Franklin County. Captain, George P Conger; First Lieut., William M. Braman; Second Lieut., Joel P. Clark.

Co. C, Washington County. Captain, William Wells; First Lieut., Henry M. Paige; Second Lieut., Eli Holden.

Co. D, Orange County. Captain, Addison W Preston; First Lieut., John W. Bennett; Second Lieut., William G. Cummings.

Co. E, Windsor County. Captain, Samuel P. Rundlett; First Lieut., Andrew J. Grover; Second Lieut., John C. Holmes.

Co. F, Windham County. Captain, Josiah Hall; First Lieut., Robert Schofield, Jr.; Second Lieut., Nathaniel E. Hayward.

Co. G, Bennington County. Captain, James A. Sheldon; First Lieut., George H. Bean; Second Lieut., Dennis M. Blackmer.

Co. H, Rutland County. Captain, Selah G. Perkins; First Lieut., Franklin T. Huntoon; Second Lieut., Charles A. Adams.

Co. I, Lamoille and Orleans Counties. Captain, Edward B. Sawyer; First Lieut., Henry C. Flint; Second Lieut., Josiah Grout, Jr.

Co. K, Addison County. Captain, Franklin Moore; First Lieut., John S. Ward; Second Lieut., John Williamson.

The field officers of the regiment were, Colonel, Lemuel B. Platt; Lieut. Colonel, George B. Kellogg; Major, William D. Collins. This regiment rendezvoused at Burlington, and was mustered into the United States service on the 19th of November, with nine hundred and sixty-six officers and men, and left the State for the seat of war on the 14th of December, 1861.

NINTH REGIMENT.

The field officers of this regiment, and the location of the companies, and the names of their commanders, were as follows: —

Colonel, George J. Stannard; Lieut. Colonel, Dudley K. Andross; Major, E. S. Stowell.

Co. A, Swanton. Captain, Valentine G. Barney.
Co. B, Rutland. Captain, Edward H. Ripley.
Co. C, Middlebury. Captain, Albert R. Sabin.
Co. D, Weathersfield. Captain, Charles Jarvis.
Co. E, Irasburg. Captain, Amasa Bartlett.
Co. F. Burlington. Captain, George A. Bebee.
Co. G, Bradford. Captain, William J. Henderson.
Co. H, Hydepark. Captain, Abel H. Slayton.
Co. I, Plainfield. Captain, Albion J. Mower.
Co. K, Brattleboro'. Captain, David W Lewis.

The Ninth Regiment rendezvoused at Brattleboro', and was mustered into the United States service on the 9th of July, 1862, with nine hundred and twenty officers and men, and left the State for the seat of war on the 15th of the same month.

This regiment was a part of the eleven thousand and five hundred men disgracefully, and, it was feared, treacherously, surrendered by Colonel Miles — an experienced regular army officer — to Stonewall Jackson, at Harper's Ferry, on the 15th of September, 1862. They were paroled and sent to Chicago, but not exchanged until the following December.

On the 18th of June, 1862, the Secretary of War telegraphed Governor Holbrook that the Government was in pressing need of troops, and inquired how many could be forwarded immediately. On the 26th he requested the Governor to raise and organize the Tenth Regiment. On the 1st of July President Lincoln issued a call for three hundred thousand volunteers, to serve for three years. The officers of the State of Vermont earnestly desired to comply as speedily as possible with the call of the President, and they were heartily seconded by her patriotic people. The work of recruiting was commenced at once, and was pressed with great energy. The Governor issued an address calling upon the people for their earnest and active co-operation in raising the Tenth and Eleventh Regiments. Eighteen recruiting offices were opened in the State; and on the 15th of August more than the number of men required for these two regiments were in camp at Brattleboro'.

GREAT REBELLION. 77

The companies composing the Tenth Regiment were as follows:—

Co. A, St. Johnsbury. Captain, Edwin B. Frost.
Co. B, Waterbury. Captain, Edwin Dillingham.
Co. C, Rutland. Captain, John A. Sheldon.
Co. D, Burlington. Captain, Giles F. Appleton.
Co. E, Bennington. Captain, Madison E. Winslow.
Co. F, Swanton. Captain, Hiram Platt.
Co. G, Bradford. Captain, George B. Damon.
Co. H, Ludlow. Captain, Levi T. Hunt.
Co. I, St. Albans. Captain, Charles G. Chandler.
Co. K, Derby Line. Captain, Hiram R. Steele.

The field officers of this regiment were, Colonel, Albert Jewett; Lieut. Colonel, John H. Edson; Major, William W. Henry.

The companies of the Eleventh Regiment were as follows:—

Co. A, St. Johnsbury. Captain, George E. Chamberlin.
Co. B, Stoneham. Captain, Charles Hunsden.
Co. O, Fairhaven. Captain, James T. Hyde.
Co. D, Hydepark. Captain, Urban A. Woodbury.
Co. E, Brattleboro'. Captain, John Hunt.
Co. F, Irasburg. Captain, James Rice.
Co. G, Bellows Falls. Captain, Charles Buxton.
Co. H, Royalton. Captain, James D. Rice.
Co. I, Worcester. Captain, Robinson Templeton.

Co. K, Alburg. Captain, George D. Sowles.

The field officers of this regiment were James M. Warner, Colonel; Reuben C. Benton, Lieut. Colonel; George E. Chamberlin, Major.

Both of these regiments were mustered into the United States service on the 1st of September; the Tenth numbering ten hundred and sixteen officers and men, and the Eleventh ten hundred and eighteen. The Tenth left the State for the seat of war on the 6th, and the Eleventh on the 7th, of September.

While the Tenth and Eleventh Regiments were being raised, urgent calls were made by the Secretary of War and the General-in-Chief of the army for recruits to fill the ranks of the regiments in the service decimated by the privations, toils, and hardships of the Peninsular Campaign. To this end each town in the State was assigned its quota, estimated on its population at the rate of thirty recruits to each thousand of population. The Adjutant General's Report of November 1, 1862, says, "For the purpose of filling the regiments in service, four thousand two hundred men were assessed upon the several towns in the State, allowing three thousand for the Ninth, Tenth, and Eleventh Regiments, and one thousand two hundred for the old regiments; and in determining the quota of each town, those towns that were deficient in their due proportion of men raised under the first call for five hundred thousand men, were charged with the deficiency, as shown by the lister's returns in April, and the sum of the deficiencies deducted from the four thousand two hundred men required, and the residue only assessed upon all the towns; thus reducing the quota of the towns not deficient from fourteen upon each thousand of population to eight upon each thousand." By an order from the Governor, the Selectmen of each town were authorized to act as recruiting officers for the purpose of raising the required number of men. Most of the towns furnished the full number required of them, while some furnished an excess beyond their quota. By an order of the War Department, the men thus enlisted were allowed to select the regiment in which they desired to serve. This resulted in raising eleven hundred and three recruits, who entered old regiments.

Under an act of Congress of July 17, 1862, allowing one additional squadron to each regiment of cavalry, two companies were raised. Co. L, consisting of one hundred and four officers and men, was mustered into the United States service on the 29th of September, 1862. Co. M consisted of one hundred and one officers and men, and was mustered into the service on the 30th of December, 1862. Both companies left the State to join the First Vermont Cavalry Regiment, at the front, soon after being mustered.

On the 4th of August, 1862, the President made a requisition for three hundred thousand militia to serve for nine months, the quota of Vermont being assessed at four thousand eight hundred and ninety-eight men. At the same time, the Secretary of War announced that if any State should not furnish its quota of three hundred thousand volunteers before the 15th of that month, the deficiency in such State would be made up by a special draft from the milita. On the 16th the Secretary of War ordered that volunteers to fill up the old regiments should be received and paid the bounty and advance pay offered by the Government until the first day of September, and for want of volunteers, a special draft would be ordered to make up the deficiency.

The publication of these orders resulted in a sudden and unexampled increase in the number of daily enlistments. The Tenth and Eleventh Regiments were rapidly filled up, and recruiting for the old regiments progressed with much credit to the patriotism of the young men of the State, who showed great determination and zeal, from first to last, to sustain the Government.

On the 11th of August, a new enrollment of all able-bodied male citizens between the ages of eighteen and forty-five years was ordered by the Adjutant General, to be made by the listers of the several towns, the rolls to be completed and returned, one copy to the town clerk, and another to the adjutant-general's office, on or before the 25th day of that month.

On the 12th of August an order was issued calling into actual service all the companies of active militia then in the State. There were upon the adjutant-general's books twenty-two of these companies, ten of which had been in the service three months, composing the first regiment, many of whom, with members of other companies, had already enlisted, and were in the service for three years; so that but six companies remained in the State, which had preserved their full and perfect organizations, and these with reduced ranks. Such was the law of the State that no legal draft could be made from enrolled militia that had been called into the service.

Fourteen uniform companies of the active militia responded to the call, with full ranks, and were mustered into the service of the United States. They were as follows: —

Allen Grays, of Brandon.
Saxton's River Light Infantry, of Rockingham.
West Windsor Guards, of West Windsor.
Woodstock Light Infantry, of Woodstock.
Bradford Guards, of Bradford.
Rutland Light Guard, of Rutland.

Howard Guards, of Burlington.
Tunbridge Light Infantry, of Tunbridge.
Ransom Guards, of St. Albans.
New England Guards, of Northfield.
Emmett Guards, of Burlington.
Frontier Guards, of Coventry.
Lafayette Artillery, of Calais.

The remaining companies of the uniform militia had either been disbanded by general orders or practically ceased to exist as organized companies previous to the order calling them into active service, so that the entire uniform militia of the State had been placed at the disposal of the government.

In compliance with an order issued on the 13th of August, providing for the enlistment of the enrolled militia by companies, through the efforts of the selectmen of the several towns in the State, and the co-operation of patriotic citizens, thirty-seven companies were enlisted, organized, offered themselves, and were accepted for nine months' service, as follows: —

Montpelier Company, from Montpelier, Waterbury, Barre, Berlin, Middlesex, and other towns.

Moretown Company, from Waitsfield, Warren, Fayston, Duxbury, Moretown, and Middlesex.

Bethel Company, from Bethel, Stockbridge, Rochester, Royalton, and Pittsfield.

Bennington Company, from Bennington, Pownal, and Woodford.

Wallingford Company, from Danby, Pawlet, Middleton, Clarendon, Wallingford, Shrewsbury, Tinmouth, and other towns.

Brattleboro' Company, from Brattleboro', Marlboro', Putney, Dummerston, Guilford, and Westminster.

Manchester Company, from Manchester, Rupert, Winhall, Sunderland, Arlington, and Dorset.

St. Johnsbury Company, from St. Johnsbury, Waterbury, Barnet, Kirby, Concord, and Ryegate.

East Montpelier Company, from East Montpelier, Berlin, Calais, Marshfield, Worcester, Plainfield, and Orange.

Ludlow Company, from Ludlow, Plymouth, Andover, Weston, Landgrove, Cavendish, and other towns.

Shoreham Company, from Shoreham, Cornwall, Bridport, Benson, Orwell, and other towns.

Townshend Company, from Wardsboro', Londonderry, Windham, Grafton, Townshend, and Jamaica.

Middlebury Company, from Middlebury, Salisbury, Addison, Cornwall, Whiting, Shoreham, Weybridge, Ripton, and other towns.

West Fairlee Company, from Vershire, Thetford, Strafford, West Fairlee, and Washington.

Springfield Company, from Springfield, Chester, Weathersfield, and Reading.

Barton Company, from Barton, Irasburg, Sutton, Albany, Craftsbury, Greensboro', Brownington, Westmore, and Glover.

Castleton Company, from Castleton, Hubbardton, Fairhaven, Poultney, and West Haven.

Wilmington Company, from Wilmington, Whitingham, Dover, Scarsboro', and Halifax.

Barnard Company, from Barnard, Pomfret, Sharon, Bridgewater, and Hartford.

Colchester Company, from Colchester, Milton, and other towns.

Bristol Company, from Bristol, Starksboro', Monkton, New Haven, Hinesburg, and other towns.

Danville Company, from Danville, Hardwick, and Walden.

Morristown Company, from Morristown, Stowe, Cambridge, Eden, Wolcott, Johnson, and Westford.

Richmond Company, from Richmond, Jericho, Underhill, Essex, St. George, Bolton, Williston, Huntington, and Starksboro'.

Rutland Company, from Rutland, Sherburne, Mendon, Chittenden, Pittsfield, Mount Holly, Ira, and other towns.

West Randolph Company, from Northfield, Brookfield, and Randolph.

Highgate Company, from Swanton, Highgate, Franklin, Grand Isle, Alburg, North Hero, South Hero, and other towns.

Bakersfield Company, from Berkshire, Bakersfield, Enosboro', Richford, Montgomery, and other towns. .

Chester Company, from Springfield, Baltimore, Weathersfield, Grafton, Cavendish, Norwich, and Chester.

Wait's River Company, from Barre, Orange, Topsham, Newbury, Groton, Corinth, Washington, Bradford, and other towns.

Island Pond Company, raised in Brighton, Holland, Morgan, Newark, Burke, Lunenburg, Canaan, East Haven, Lemington, Charleston, Brunswick, and Maidstone.

Vergennes Company, raised in Charlotte, Addison, Vergennes, Ferrisburg, New Haven, Huntington, Goshen, Panton, and Granville.

McIndoe's Falls Company, raised in Barnet, Peacham, Ryegate, Danville, Coventry, Greensboro', Barton, Waterford, and St. Johnsbury.

Lyndon Company, raised in Sheffield, Wheelock, Lyndon, Sutton, Glover, Guildhall, Kirby, and Victory.

Danby Company, raised in Danby, Pownal, Rupert, Sandgate, Shaftsbury, Stamford, Wallingford, Wells, Poultney, and other towns.

Felchville Company, raised in Reading, Hartford, Hartland, Weston, Royalton, Barnard, Sharon, Stockbridge, Windsor, and other towns.

Williamstown Company, raised in Newfane, Putney, Guilford, Peru, Stratton, Readsboro', Dummerston, Brookline, Searsburg, Windham, Wardsboro', Marlboro', Jamaica, and other towns.

A draft was ordered to make up deficiencies in the quotas of the several towns in the State, to take place on the 10th of September, 1862. Before that time the quotas had been so far filled that but fifty men were drafted in all. Many of these enlisted, others were thrown out by the medical inspector, and the balance furnished substitutes. The ultimate result was, that the State furnished five full regiments under the call of the President.

These several companies were organized into regiments, as follows: —

Twelfth Regiment.

Co. A, West Windsor Guards. Captain, Charles L. Savage.

Co. B, Woodstock Light Infantry. Captain, Ora Paul, Jr.

Co. C, Howard Guards. Captain, Leonard W Page.

Co. D, Tunbridge Light Infantry. Captain, David F. Cole.

Co. E, Ransom Guards. Captain, Hamilton S. Gilbert.

Co. F, New England Guards. Captain, Darius Thomas.

Co. G, Allen Grays. Captain, Ebenezer J. Ormsbee.

Co. H, Bradford Guards. Captain, Preston S. Chamberlin.

Co. I, Saxton's River Light Infantry. Captain, Carlton H. Roundy.

Co. K, Rutland Light Guard. Captain, Walter C. Landon.

The field officers of this regiment were, Asa P. Blunt, Colonel; Roswell Farnham, Lieut. Colonel; Levi C. Kingsley, Major. It was mustered into the United States service at Brattleboro', with nine hundred and eighty-eight officers and men, on the 4th, and left the State on the 7th of October.

THIRTEENTH REGIMENT.

Co. A, Emmett Guards. Captain, John Lanergan.

Co. B, Moretown Company. Captain, Oscar C. Wilder.

Co. C, East Montpelier Company. Captain, Lewis L. Colburn.

Co. D, Colchester Company. Captain, William D. Munson.

Co. E, Morristown Company. Captain, Joseph J. Boynton.

Co. F, Richmond Company. Captain, John L. Yale.

Co. G, Bakersfield Company. Captain, Marvin White.

Co. H, Lafayette Artillery. Captain, William V Peck.

Co. I, Montpelier Company. Captain, John M. Thacher.

Co. K, Highgate Company. Captain, George S. Blake.

The field officers of this regiment were, William T. Nichols, Colonel; Charles W. Rose, Lieut. Colonel; Nathaniel B. Hall, Major. It was mustered into the United States service at Brattleboro', with nine hundred and fifty-three officers and men, on the 10th, and left the State on the 11th of October.

Fourteenth Regiment.

Co. A, Bennington Company. Captain, Ransom O. Gore.

Co. B, Wallingford Company. Captain, John C. Thompson.

Co. C, Manchester Company. Captain, Josiah B. Munson.

Co. D, Shoreham Company. Captain, Charles E. Abell.

Co. E, Middlebury Company. Captain, Edwin Rich.

Co. F, Castleton Company. Captain, Joseph Jennings.

Co. G, Bristol Company. Captain, Noble F. Dunshee.

Co. H, Rutland Company. Captain, Walter C. Dunton.

Co. I, Vergennes Company. Captain, Solomon T. Allen.

Co. K, Danby Company. Captain, Alonzo N. Colvin.

The field officers were, William T. Nichols, Colonel; Charles W. Rose, Lieut. Colonel; Nathaniel B. Hall, Major. It was mustered into the United States service at Brattleboro', with nine hundred and fifty-two officers and men, on the 21st, and left the State on the 22d of October.

FIFTEENTH REGIMENT.

Co. A, West Fairlee Company. Captain, Horace E. Brown.

Co. B, Danville Company. Captain, James M. Ayer.

Co. C, West Randolph Company. Captain, C. N. Carpenter.

Co. D, Wait's River Company. Captain, Charles G. French.

Co. E, Island Pond Company. Captain, Warren Noyes.

Co. F, McIndoe's Falls Company. Captain, Xerxes C. Stevens.

Co. G, Lyndon Company. Captain, Stephen McGaffey.

Co. H, Frontier Guards. Captain, Riley E. Wright.

Co. I, Barton Company. Captain, William H. Johnson.

Co. K, St. Johnsbury Company. Captain, George B. Woodward.

The field officers were, Redfield Proctor, Colonel; William W Grout, Lieut. Colonel; Charles F. Spalding, Major. It was mustered into the United States service at Brattleboro', with nine hundred and thirty-five officers and men, on the 22d, and left the State on the 23d of October.

SIXTEENTH REGIMENT.

Co. A, Bethel Company. Captain, Henry A. Eaton.

Co. B, Brattleboro' Company. Captain, Robert B. Arms.

Co. C, Ludlow Company. Captain, Asa G. Foster.

Co. D, Townshend Company. Captain, David Ball.

Co. E, Springfield Company. Captain, Alvin C. Mason.

Co. F, Wilmington Company. Captain, Henry F. Dix.

Co. G, Barnard Company. Captain, Harvey N. Bruce.

Co. H, Felchville Company. Captain, Joseph C. Sawyer.

Co. I, Williamsville Company. Captain, Lyman E. Knapp.

Co. K, Chester Company. Captain, Samuel Hutchinson.

The field officers were, Wheelock G. Veazey, Colonel; Charles Cummings, Lieut. Colonel; William

Rounds, Major. It was mustered into the United States service at Brattleboro', with nine hundred and forty-nine officers and men, on the 23d, and left the State on the 24th of October.

When the muster of the foregoing five regiments was completed, there were in the service from Vermont fifteen regiments of Infantry, one regiment of Cavalry, two batteries of Light Artillery, and three companies of Sharpshooters. According to the Adjutant General's Report, the account stood with the State as follows: —

Men furnished on first requisition for 500,000 men,					9,283
"	"	" second "		" 300,000 "	4,164
"	"	" third "		" 300,000 "	4,777
	Total,				18,224

On the 1st of November, 1862, there were in the field from the State of Vermont fifteen regiments of Infantry, one regiment of Cavalry, two batteries of Light Artillery, and three companies of Sharpshooters, then numbering over sixteen thousand officers and men. Of these, five regiments of infantry were enlisted for nine months, and the residue for three years or during the war.

In December, 1862, the Eleventh Infantry Regiment was, by order of the War Department, changed to Heavy Artillery, and an additional company was raised for it and mustered into the United States service July

11, 1863, with one hundred and fifty-one officers and men. Subsequently another company was enlisted, organized, and added to this regiment. An additional company was raised, consisting of one hundred and one officers and men, mustered into the United States service December 30, 1862, and added to the First Regiment of Cavalry. A brigade band, of fifteen men, for the brigade composed of the old regiments from the State, was enlisted and mustered into the service May 26, 1863.

In October, 1863, the State stood credited by the War Department with one hundred and twenty-eight men in excess of her quota under all calls for troops which had then been made.

The term of service of the Twelfth, Thirteenth, Fourteenth, Fifteenth, and Sixteenth Regiments, enlisted for nine months, having expired, they were mustered out from the 14th of July to the 10th of August, 1863.

Under an order of the War Department, drafts were made from the enrolled militia of the State by Congressional districts. That in the Third District took place on the 26th of September; Second District, 30th of September; and First District, 1st of October, 1863. The quota assigned to the State, to be raised by draft, was 4715. The whole number of men drafted was 7071; accepted, 2781; entered the service, 318; procured substitutes, 630 ; paid commutation, 1833 ; making a total of men who entered the service, furnished substitutes, and paid commutation, of 2781, leaving a deficiency of 1934 men, to be raised by supplemental draft, or otherwise furnished by the State. The men obtained by the draft were most of them sent to fill up the old regiments, depleted by casualties of field and camp. The deficiency was made up by enlistments induced by the spirit of patriotism which pervaded the State from the beginning to the close of the war, and by the large bounties and pay offered by towns, State, and United States.

During the year from October 1, 1863, to October 1, 1864, under a general order of the War Department authorizing the re-enlistment of men in the service who had less than one year of their original term of enlistment to serve, and offering a bounty and premium of four hundred and two dollars to all who should thus re-enlist, one thousand nine hundred and forty-three men re-enlisted in regiments and detached companies from Vermont.

The term of service of the Second Regiment expired June 19, 1864, and on the 22d it was mustered out of service at Brattleboro', with two hundred and nineteen officers and men. The term of the Third expired July 15, 1864, and it was mustered out at Burlington on the 27th, with one hundred and sixty officers and men. The term of the Fourth expired September 20, 1864, and it was mustered out at Brattleboro' on the 30th, with one hundred and forty-six officers and men. The term of the Fifth expired September 15, 1864, but its organization was preserved by the re-enlistment of the requisite number of men. Such as had not re-enlisted were mustered out as a detachment in the field, and returned to Burlington to be paid. The term of the Sixth expired October 14, 1864, but preserved its organization by re-enlistments, and was mustered out June 26, 1865. The term of the Seventh expired February 12, 1865, but it was not mustered out until March 14th, 1866. The other infantry served until after the close of the war. The First Company of Sharpshooters was mustered out September 13, 1864; the Second, November 9, 1864; the Third, December 30, 1861. The First Light Battery was mustered out August 10, 1864; the Second, September 20, 1864; the Third served to the end of the war. The First Regiment of Cavalry was mustered out of service November 18, 1864.

VERMONT TROOPS.

During the four years' existence of the War of the Rebellion — from the first assault upon Fort Sumter, April 12, 1861, to the surrender of Lee's army at Appomattox Court House, April 9, 1865 — all the Free States acted well their parts. New England, whose sentiments with regard to the peculiar institution, and the great interest of the South, had been for years misunderstood, and persistently misrepresented by senators and representatives in Congress, by the newspaper press, and by the influential men generally in and from the Slave States, was especially hated for her thrift, enterprise, and intelligence. Her senators and representatives had been insulted, bullied, and assaulted upon the floor of Congress. She had been defied, and the patriotism and bravery of her sons had been called in question; and when the flag of the common country was fired upon by South Carolina, every New England man felt insulted, and called upon to protect and defend it, if need be with his life, his property, and his sacred honor.

Vermont participated largely in this feeling, and immediately on the reception of the call of President Lincoln for seventy-five thousand volunteers for three months, Governor Fairbanks called the Legislature to assemble, and take all needed measures to put into the field her quota of men. On the 23d of April the Legislature assembled at Montpelier, and Governor Fairbanks delivered before the joint assembly the following practical and patriotic address: —

"*Gentlemen of the Senate and House of Representatives:*—

"We are convened to-day in view of events of an extraordinary and very alarming character. The element of disunion, which, in a portion of the United States, for many years, vented itself in threats and menaces, has culminated in open rebellion; and an unnatural and causeless civil war has been precipitated against the general government.

"Unprincipled and ambitious men have organized a despotism and an armed force for the purpose of overthrowing that government which the American people have formed for themselves, and of destroying that constitutional framework under which we have enjoyed peace and prosperity, and from a small and feeble people grown and expanded to a rank among the first nations of the earth.

"The enormity of this rebellion is heightened by the consideration that no valid cause exists for it. The history of the civilized world does not furnish an instance where a revolution was attempted for such slight causes. No act of oppression, no attempted or threatened invasion of the rights of the revolting States, has existed, either on the part of the general government or of the loyal States; but the principle has been recognized and observed, that the right of each and every State to regulate its domestic institutions should remain inviolate.

"The inception and progress of this rebellion have been remarkable, and characterized at every stage by a total absence of any high honorable principle or motive in its leaders.

"Its master spirits are composed, essentially, of men who have been in high official position in the general government; and it has transpired that members of the late Cabinet at Washington, while in the exercise of their official functions, were engaged in treasonable plots for seizing the public property and subverting the United States government.

"Conventions of delegates in the revolting States, chosen, in some instances, by a minority of the legal voters of those States, have, with indecent haste, adopted ordinances of secession, which ordinances have in no instance been submitted to the people for their ratification.

"These proceedings have been followed by a convention of delegates from the several revolting States, which convention has organized a confederate government, adopted a constitution, elected its executive officers and subordinate functionaries, constituted itself into a legislative body, and enacted a code of laws, — all which proceedings have been independent of any action of the people of those States.

"The authorities of the revolting States, and subsequently that of their confederacy, have proceeded to acts of robbery and theft upon the property of the United States within their limits. Forts, arsenals, arms, military stores, and other public property, have been seized and appropriated for use against the power of the general government; and custom-houses and mints in Southern cities, with large amounts of treasure, have been feloniously robbed.

"These acts have been followed by military demonstrations and strategetical operations against the United States forts at Pensacola and Charleston, the latter of which, under its gallant commander, Major Anderson, after a bombardment of thirty-four hours, from beleaguering batteries of the insurgents, was evacuated on the 13th instant, and the flag of the Union withdrawn. But the crowning act of perfidy, on the part of the conspirators, is the proclamation of Jefferson Davis, styling himself the President of the Southern Confederacy, 'inviting all those who may desire, by service in private-armed vessels on the high seas, to aid his government, to make application for commissions, or letters of marque or reprisal;' thus instituting a grand scheme of piracy on the high seas against the lives and private property of peaceful citizens.

"These acts of outrage and daring rebellion have

been equaled only by the forbearance of the general government. Unwilling to precipitate a conflict which must involve the country in all the calamities of civil war, the present government of the United States has exhausted every effort for peace, and every measure for bringing back to their allegiance these disaffected and misguided States.

"The duty of protecting the forts and government property, not possessed by the insurgents, was imperative upon the administration; but further than this, no measures for coercing the revolting States into obedience to the constitution and the laws were adopted, and in the matter of the beleaguered forts, the government acted only on the defensive, until the conflict was commenced by the insurgents.

"Such forbearance on the part of the government, while it has served to place the conspirators in a moral wrong, is no longer justifiable; and the country hails with entire unanimity and with ardent enthusiasm the decision of the President to call into requisition the whole power of the nation for suppressing the rebellion, and repelling threatened aggressions.

"From every part of the country, in all the loyal States, there is one united voice for sustaining the Union, the Constitution, and the integrity of the United States government. All partisan differences are ignored and lost in the higher principles of patriotism.

"In this patriotic enthusiasm Vermont eminently participates. Her citizens, always loyal to the Union, will, in this hour of peril, nobly rally for the protection of the government and the constitution.

"On the fifteenth instant, the President of the United States issued his proclamation, 'calling forth the militia of the several States of the Union, to the aggregate number of seventy-five thousand, in order to suppress treasonable combinations, and cause the laws to be duly executed.'

"The quota required of Vermont, for immediate service, is one regiment of seven hundred and eighty officers and privates.

"On receiving the requisition from the Secretary of War for this regiment, I ordered the adjutant and inspector general to adopt the proper measures for calling into service such of the volunteer companies as are necessary to make up the complement; and the quartermaster general was directed to procure, with the least possible delay, the requisite outfit of knapsacks, overcoats, blankets, and other equipments; which duty he has performed.

"Having adopted the foregoing preliminary measures for responding to the call of the President, I availed myself of the constitutional provision for convening the general assembly of an extra session, not doubting that you, gentlemen, representing the universally expressed patriotism of the citizens of this State, will make all necessary appropriations and provisions for defraying the expenses already incurred, and carrying into execution further measures for placing our military quota at the service of the general government.

"Conceiving it imminently probable that, at an early day, further calls may be made upon this State for troops, I respectfully call your attention to the importance of adopting immediate measures for a more efficient organization of the military arm of the State.

"During the long interval of peace which we have enjoyed, while our citizens have been uninterrupted in their lawful industrial pursuits, the importance of a military organization and discipline has been lost sight of. Our laws in relation to the militia have been subjected, during nearly a quarter of a century, to numerous isolated amendments and alterations, until, as a code, they are disjointed, complicated, and altogether too cumbrous for the basis of a regular and effective organization. I therefore recommend that the Legislature should promptly remedy these defects, and adopt such enactments as shall provide effectively for organizing, arming, and equipping the militia of the State, and for reasonably compensating the officers and privates when required to meet for exercise and drill.

"I desire also to urge upon you the duty of making contingent appropriations of money, to be expended, under the direction of the Executive, for the outfit of any additional military forces which may be called for by the general government.

"The occasion is an extraordinary one. Intelligence reaches us that the Virginia convention of delegates, elected under the express provision that any ordinance adopted by them should be submitted to the people for their approval or rejection, has, in secret session, passed an ordinance of secession, and that the Governor of the State has assumed to order the seizure of the United States forts, arsenals, and vessels within the limits of that State.

"The Federal capital is menaced by an imposing and well-armed military force, and the government itself, and the national archives, are in imminent peril.

"Such is the emergency, in view of which I invoke your immediate action. The Legislatures of other States have made liberal appropriations and extensive military arrangements for aiding the government, and their citizens are hastening to the rescue of our country's flag. We shall discredit our past history should we, in this crisis, suffer Vermont to be behind her sister States in her patriotic sacrifices for the preservation of the Union and the constitution.

"I feel assured, gentlemen, that you will best reflect the sentiments and wishes of your constituents, by emulating in your legislative action the patriotism and liberality of the noble States which have already responded to the call of the government.

"It is devoutly to be hoped that the mad ambition of the secession leaders may be restrained, and the impending sanguinary conflict averted. But a hesitating, half-way policy on the part of the administration of the loyal States will not avail to produce such a result.

"The United States government must be sustained, and the rebellion suppressed, at whatever cost of men and treasure; and it remains to be seen whether the vigorous preparations that are being made, and the immense military force called into service by the President, are not the most probable and certain measures for a speedy and successful solution of the question.

"May the Divine Being, who rules among the nations, and directs the affairs of men, interpose by his merciful providence, and restore to us again the blessing of peace, under the ægis of our national constitution."

This call of the Governor for prompt and efficient action by the Legislature of Vermont was not made in vain. He did not misjudge the patriotism of the people, or the willingness of their representatives to render all needed aid to the government for the protection of her beloved flag and the upholding of the laws. No time was spent in useless discussion as to the precise way that succor should be given to the Executive of the nation, but acts were immediately passed appropriating one million dollars for arming, equipping, and holding, subject to orders from the War Department, the militia of the State, and doing other things to send promptly to the field any required troops, pay them a fair equivalent for their services while fighting the battles of the country, and taking care of the dear ones they should leave behind them. The Legislature placed the responsibility of raising, organizing, uniforming, arming, equipping, and subsisting the regiments in the hands of the Governor, giving him authority to draw his warrants on the State Treasurer for all expenditures.

All this was done, and the Legislature adjourned on the 27th of April, four days after assembling. The promptness and decisive energy of that body of lawgivers was an example for every young man in the State to imitate, by enrolling himself "for the war;" and most nobly and patriotically did they do it. Almost every farm, workshop, mill, counting-room, and office in the State sent forth to the field its representative; and many of them, alas! never returned.

During the whole four years' continuance of the war, Vermont was ever ready with her men and her treasure to aid the government whenever and however called upon. Such was the character of her population that a greater percentage of native-born citizens was sent than from any other State, and the reputation of her troops for bravery, endurance, and intelligence was deservedly very high.

When the war first broke out, it was presumed that other troops than those required to fill her share of the seventy-five thousand first called for by the President might be needed from Vermont before the rebellion, the proportions of which were very little understood, should be suppressed; and it was supposed that should she send three full regiments, and keep their constantly decimating ranks filled by new enlistments, she would be taxed to the extent of her capacity. In the four years, however, she furnished eighteen regiments, three batteries, and three detached companies. The original enlistments, and the recruits sent forward to the several organizations to fill their decimated ranks, from time to time, made an aggregate of 34,238 men, at an expense to the State of $9,087,353.40, of which the sum of $5,215,787.70 was expended by the several towns, in their municipal capacity, without expectation of repayment.

Of these 34,238 men enlisted, 5124 were killed, and died of wounds. and disease contracted in the service, and 5022 were discharged from the service before the expiration of their term of enlistment, by reason of disability. The late adjutant general, in his report, gives the total loss in all the various forms of casualty, at 13,724 officers and men.

When we have these facts of the number of troops furnished, the lives lost, physical constitutions broken down, and money expended by the small State of Vermont, and remember that other States did their share as well, we can make some sort of a just estimate of the total cost in life and treasure to the loyal States of the four years of the Great Rebellion. And yet such are the resources and the recuperative powers of the loyal States that after four years of peace we have but few reminders of the sanguinary struggle left, except here and there a vacant place by the family hearthstone; an occasional empty sleeve; a missing leg. left upon the battle-field; innumerable scarred veterans halting by us, carrying about with them unmistakable evidence of many well-fought battles; and a small increase of public rates.

The history of the services of the Vermont regiments in the field — the battles in which they engaged and the sieges they passed — is yet to be written. Here they can have but a passing notice. They can be rewarded for their hardships and sacrifices only by the consciousness of duty to their country well and nobly performed.

First Regiment.

This regiment was enlisted for three months, but in that time did just the service that was required at that stage of the war. They were engaged in several reconnoissances, and one severe battle, — that of Big Bethel, — in which they behaved bravely. The following is the report of the commanding officer of the regiment in that engagement: —

"CAMP BUTLER, AT NEWPORT NEWS, VA.,
June 11, 1861.

"To J. W. PHELPS, *Colonel First Regiment Vermont Volunteers, commanding the Post.*

"SIR: Pursuant to your order, I left camp between twelve and one o'clock on the morning of the 10th, with five companies of the Vermont Regiment, being the 2d Co., Captain Pelton; the 4th Co., Captain Andros; the 6th Co., Captain Boynton; the 8th Co., Captain Peck; and the 10th Co., Captain Ripley; and five companies of the Fourth Massachusetts Regiment, being Co. F, Captain Shepard; Co. G, Captain Gordon; Co. H, Captain Curtis; Co. K, Captain Barnes, and Co. M (rifles), Captain Clark. The strength of the command was, Vermont Regiment, 13 officers and 262 men; Massachusetts Regiment, 15 officers and 248 men, making a total of 28 officers and 510 men.

"Colonel Benedix, with a detachment of the Seventh New York Volunteers, followed my detachment, with two field-pieces and eleven artillerists, under the command of Lieutenant Greble, of the Second Artillery. The march proceeded quietly, and with great dispatch, until we were within about half a mile of Little Bethel, — our place of designation, — Colonel Benedix having halted with his detachment and one field-piece, at the junction of the road from Newport News with the road from Hampton, and Lieutenant Greble having followed in the rear of my detachment with one gun. While continuing the march, heavy firing of small arms was heard in our rear, in the direction of Colonel Benedix's detachment. When it had continued so long and sharply that it appeared to me that it was a serious attack, I countermarched my troops and returned to the place where Colonel Benedix was stationed, and found that he was opposed by a large body of troops, coming from the direction of Hampton, a portion of whom I could then see upon a rise of land in front. I immediately formed my command in order of battle, and then, fearing that they were our friends, I caused my whole line to shout 'Boston!' together, four times. Receiving no response, I advanced my line, and was fired upon from a howitzer, the fire doing us no injury. The enemy, as I then supposed them to be, then disappeared, and I went forward to a house near by, where I found a number of wounded men, who stated that they belonged to Colonel Townshend's New York Regiment. At this time Colonel Duryea, with his regiment, who had also heard the firing, and who had reached Little Bethel at about the same time that I should have reached that place if my march had not been interrupted, came to the same place, and General Pierce, who had been with Colonel Townshend's regiment, also came up. General Pierce then assumed command of all the troops, and by his order I moved my detachment on to Great Bethel. The enemy we found there, intrenched in force. Pursuant to the orders of the general, I formed my troops in line of battle, in rear of Colonel Townshend's regiment. Previous to this, General Pierce had taken from my command one half of Captain Shepard's Company F, of the Fourth Massachusetts Volunteers, to guard certain stores at Little Bethel, taking three non-commissioned officers and twenty-one privates. After forming line of battle, General Pierce directed that two of my companies be detached as skirmishers, to hold the woods upon our left, and prevent a flank attack. The eighth and tenth Companies of the First Vermont Regiment were detached for that service, and were thus entirely separated from my command. Immediately afterwards, Captain Clark's rifles (Co. M), of the Fourth Massachusetts Regiment, and the residue of Captain Shepard's Company, were also detached by General Pierce and sent into the woods, to act as skirmishers in connection with Colonel Duryea's Regiment, and were thus separated from my command. I then received an order from General Pierce to move through the woods, beyond the right of the Zouaves, and attack the left flank of the enemy's battery. No other direction as to location was given, and no guide was sent with me. I moved through the woods, which were very close and tangled, and, after considerable difficulty, succeeded in placing my men in the proper position, and opened fire.

"The attack by my men was very spirited, and the firing from both sides very warm. Soon after I commenced the attack, the firing ceased upon every other part of the work, and the enemy's fire appeared to be concentrated upon us. While making the attack, I was joined by Colonel Benedix with a body of his men, probably sixty in all. After the firing had continued about twenty minutes, the enemy brought their artillery to bear upon us with grape shot; and finding that I was not supported by any fire or attack elsewhere, except an occasional fire from Lieutenant Greble's guns, I ceased firing, and withdrew my men, in good order, under cover of the woods. There the companies became separated, so that, in forming line, I found with me only Captain Pelton's Company of the First Vermont Regiment, and Captain Barnes' and Captain Curtis' Companies of the Fourth Massachusetts Regiment, and a few men from the Fourth and Sixth Companies of the Vermont Regiment. After remaining in line until all the men had come in from the point of attack, I returned with those men to the place where I had first formed. I then found that Colonel Duryea's Regiment had retired, and were then out of sight, and Colonel Townshend's Regiment were also retiring. All of my detachment assembled quietly, and I formed line of battle again upon the ground I had first occupied, and reported to General Pierce for further orders, and was told by him that he had ordered a retreat, and was directed to retire with my command. I retired about fifty rods, and then halted until the wounded had been got ready for transportation, and the two field-pieces had been brought off. One I left with General Pierce, and the other I moved off to the rear, when General Pierce informed me that the one left had been disabled, and directed me to leave the other for Colonel Allen's Regiment, to cover the retreat; and I did so. Both were taken by General Pierce to Fort Monroe. I then commenced the return march, arriving in camp toward night.

"The expedition was a most exhausting one for all under my command. In eighteen hours the men marched some thirty-five miles, and were engaged in battle with very slight rest, and no food except a little hard bread. Before commencing the battle they had been under arms nine hours without refreshment. The strength of the companies with which I made the assault upon the works was, at that time, Vermont companies, 5 officers and 148 men; Massachusetts companies, 9 officers and 127 men: total, 289. The killed, wounded, and missing were 7: viz., Vermont, 3 wounded, 1 missing; Massachusetts, 2 killed, 1 mortally wounded. Captain Andros, of Vermont, was among the wounded.

"The officers and men who were left under my immediate command behaved with perfect coolness, and kept perfect order, both in the advance through the woods and in the attack upon the works. Every one went into the engagement, and fought manfully, and without flinching. Where all behaved so well, I cannot particularize any of those under my immediate eye. It would be invidious to do so. I particularly noticed the coolness and bravery of Major Whittemore, of the Fourth Massachusetts Regiment, who was my second in command; of Captains Pelton and Andros, and Lieutenant Webb, of the Vermont Regiment; and of Captains Barnes, Curtis, and Gordon, of the Fourth Massachusetts Regiment. Captain Pelton was the first man who mounted the bank in face of the enemy, and he retained his exposed situation during most of the attack. Captain Andros reports privates A. H. Stover, George W Flanders, Burnham Caverly, and A. J. Going, of the Fourth Company of the Vermont Regiment as entitled to commendation. The other captains report that all their men behaved with so much resolution and courage that they cannot particularize any. To Major Whittemore I am much indebted for the compact order and effective position upon the march in which the men were kept. In the attack he was in the foremost lines.

"I return herewith the reports of Captains Ripley and Peck, of the Vermont Regiment, and Captains Shepard and Clark, of the Fourth Massachusetts Regiment, who were taken from under my command by General Pierce, and who were not afterward with me until the action had closed.

"I regret to be compelled to report also the death of Lieutenant Greble. He occupied, with his guns, the most exposed position in the attack, and worked them with most perfect coolness and bravery during the action. He was killed by the last discharge but one which was fired by the enemy. The men under his command are justly entitled to great credit. They fought bravely, brought off all their guns, and also the body of Lieutenant Greble. From information received by me, I particularly mention Corporal Peeples, and also private Bisgard of Company F, of the Third United States Artillery.

"From my personal observation, I believe Major Winthrop, of Major General Butler's staff, to have been killed during my attack. He came to me during the midst of the attack, and rushed forward, and one of my men, describing his uniform, appearance, and arms accurately, states that he fell by his side.

"I have the honor to remain,
"Your most obedient servant,
"PETER T. WASHBURN,
"*Lieutenant Colonel First Vermont Volunteers.*"

The following, in reference to this First Vermont Regiment, is an extract from an oration before the Reunion Society of Vermont Officers, at Montpelier, in October, 1868, by General P. T. Washburn, who was lieutenant colonel and much of the time its commander: —

"Of the First Regiment of Vermont Volunteers I must be allowed to speak with pride. They were the first to volunteer from the State. The order for their organization was issued on the 23d of April; they were in camp on the 3d of May; left the State on the 9th; bore proudly through the streets of New York the little sprig of evergreen, which designated each man as one of the noble race of Green Mountain Boys, whose fathers had fought and won at Bennington, and whose sons had maintained the integrity of their sires, until they had gained for their State the proud title of 'the Star that never sets.' They were in Fortress Monroe on the 13th, — too late to save Norfolk, with its immense armament, which treachery had surrendered to treason only a few days preceding their

arrival, — but seasonably to preserve the fortress from capture by the rebel bands which then swarmed under its very walls, and effectually blockaded every approach by land. They served faithfully their term. The name of the first battle of the war is inscribed upon their record; and when they returned to be disbanded, it was but to tender service again in other organizations, again to maintain the honor of the State and the integrity of the nation in field and camp. The history of every subsequent organization, the history of Vermont in the war, is in part their history."

The men composing this regiment were all esteemed citizens at home, and most of them left profitable business and took up arms when their country called. As the cars were leaving Rutland, one of the privates, in response to the cheers of the people, said, —

"The Vermont Regiment, citizens in peace, soldiers in war, give you the sentiment embodied in the charge of the Grecian matron to her son, 'We will bring back our shields, or be brought back upon them.'"

More than six hundred of the men who composed the First Regiment subsequently joined other organizations, and served through the war. More than two hundred and fifty of them held commissions of every grade, from second lieutenant to brigadier general. Selden Conner, who was a private in the Woodstock Company, was appointed lieutenant colonel in the

Seventh Maine Regiment, and rose to the rank of brigadier general. He was wounded in the battles of the Wilderness. Samuel H. Lincoln, private in the Woodstock Company, was afterwards colonel of the Sixth Vermont Regiment. Captain Oscar S. Tuttle, of the First, was afterward colonel of the Sixth Vermont. Lieutenant George T. Roberts, of the Rutland Company, was afterwards colonel of the Seventh Vermont Regiment. He was killed at Baton Rouge. Captain David B. Peck, of the Burlington Company, was lieutenant colonel and then colonel of the Seventh Regiment. The regiment was so much reduced in numbers that he was not mustered as colonel. Captain Dudley K. Andros, of the Bradford Company, was afterward colonel of the Ninth Regiment. Lieutenant Albert B. Jewett, of the Swanton Company, was afterward colonel of the Tenth Regiment. Private William T. Nichols, of the Rutland Company, was afterward colonel of the Fourteenth Regiment.

So much room would not be devoted to the record of this regiment but for its very remarkable history, and the fact that its period of service was a most interesting one in the great war.

VERMONT BRIGADE.

The history of the "Vermont Brigade" is honorable alike to itself and the State from which it went, whose name it bore upon its banner. In the autumn of 1862, the Second, Third, Fourth, Fifth, and Sixth Regiments, of Vermont Infantry, were brigaded together, and constituted the Second Brigade, Second Division, Sixth Corps, of the Army of the Potomac. On the 10th of May, 1864, the Eleventh Regiment was added. It acquired the distinctive name of the "Vermont Brigade," and as such did the State and whose young men composed it great honor on many hard-fought fields. It was successively commanded by Brigadier Generals W F Smith, W T. H. Brooks, Colonel Henry Whiting, and Brigadier General L. A. Grant. It participated in nearly every battle in which the army of the Potomac was engaged, and always with bravery and distinction.

The Second Regiment was successively commanded by Colonel Henry Whiting, of Michigan, a graduate of West Point, who resigned in February, 1863; James H. Walbridge, of Bennington, who resigned in April, 1864; Newton Stone, of Bennington, who was killed at the Wilderness, Virginia, May 5, 1864; John S. Tyler, of Brattleboro', who died May 23, 1864, of wounds received in the Wilderness; and Amasa S. Tracy, who was mustered out with the regiment, July 15, 1865. Before being brigaded with the other Vermont regiments, the Second took part in the battle of Bull Run, July 21, 1861.

The Third Regiment was successively commanded by Colonels William F Smith, a native of Vermont, graduate of West Point, who was promoted brigadier general of volunteers August 13, 1861; Breed N. Hyde, of Hydepark, who resigned January 15, 1863; Thomas O. Seaver, of Pomfret, who was mustered out of service July 27, 1864; and Horace W Floyd, who was mustered out with his regiment July 11, 1865. Before the formation of the Vermont Brigade, the Third Regiment participated in the battle at Lewinsville, September 11, 1861.

The Fourth Regiment was commanded by Colonels Edwin H. Stoughton, of Rockingham, a graduate of West Point, who was promoted brigadier general of volunteers November 5, 1862; Charles B. Stoughton, of Rockingham, who resigned by reason of wounds, February 2, 1864; George P. Foster, of Walden, who was breveted brigadier general August 1, 1864, for gallant and meritorious service before Richmond and in the Shenandoah Valley, and was mustered out of service with his regiment, July 13, 1865.

The Fifth Regiment was commanded by Colonels Henry A. Smalley, a native of Vermont, graduate of West Point, and captain Second United States Artillery (his leave of absence from his company was revoked September 10, 1862); Lewis A. Grant, of Rockingham, promoted brigadier general of volunteers April

27, 1864; John R. Lewis, of Burlington, wounded severely, May 5, 1864, appointed colonel of Veteran Reserve Corps breveted brigadier general of volunteers for gallant service in the battle of the Wilderness, Virginia, to date from March 13, 1865; Roland A. Kennedy, of Concord, who entered Company I, Third Regiment, as a private, in June, 1861, was wounded May 4, 1863, and was mustered out with the Fifth Regiment, June 29, 1865.

The Sixth Regiment was commanded by Nathan Lord, Jr., of Montpelier, who resigned December 18, 1862; Oscar S. Tuttle, of Cavendish, who resigned March 18, 1863; Elisha L. Barney, of Swanton, who died May 10, 1864, of wounds received in action at the Wilderness, Virginia, May 5, 1864; Sumner H. Lincoln, who was a private in Company B, was wounded May 5, 1864; mustered out with his regiment June 26, 1865.

These five regiments composed the Vermont Brigade, and they were together and participated in the same marches and battles during nearly their whole term of service. The following are the battles in which they were engaged:—

Lee's Mills,	April 16, 1862.
Williamsburg,	May 5, 1862.
Golding's Farm,	June 26, 1862.
Savage Station,	June 30 to July 2, 1862.

Crampton's Gap,   September 14, 1862.
Antietam,   September 17, 1862.
Fredericksburg,   December 13, 1862.
Mayre's Heights,   May 3, 1863.
Salem Heights,   May 4, 1863.
Fredericksburg,   June 5, 1863.
Gettysburg,   July 3, 1863.
Funkstown,   July 10, 1863.
Rappahannock Station, November 7, 1863.
Wilderness,   May 5 to 10, 1864.
Spottsylvania,   May 10 to 18, 1864.
Cold Harbor,   June 1 to 12, 1864.
Petersburg,   June 18, 1864.
Weldon Railroad,   June 23, 1864.
Charlestown,   August 21, 1864.
Opequan,   September 13, 1864.
Winchester,   September 19, 1864.
Fisher's Hill,   September 21 and 22, 1864.
Cedar Creek,   October 19, 1864.
Petersburg,   March 25 and 27, 1865.
Petersburg,   April 2, 1865.

BATTLE OF LEE'S MILLS.

The battle of Lee's Mills occurred during the siege of Yorktown, and in it the Vermont Brigade performed a conspicuous and important part. The rebels were strongly intrenched on the opposite side of the

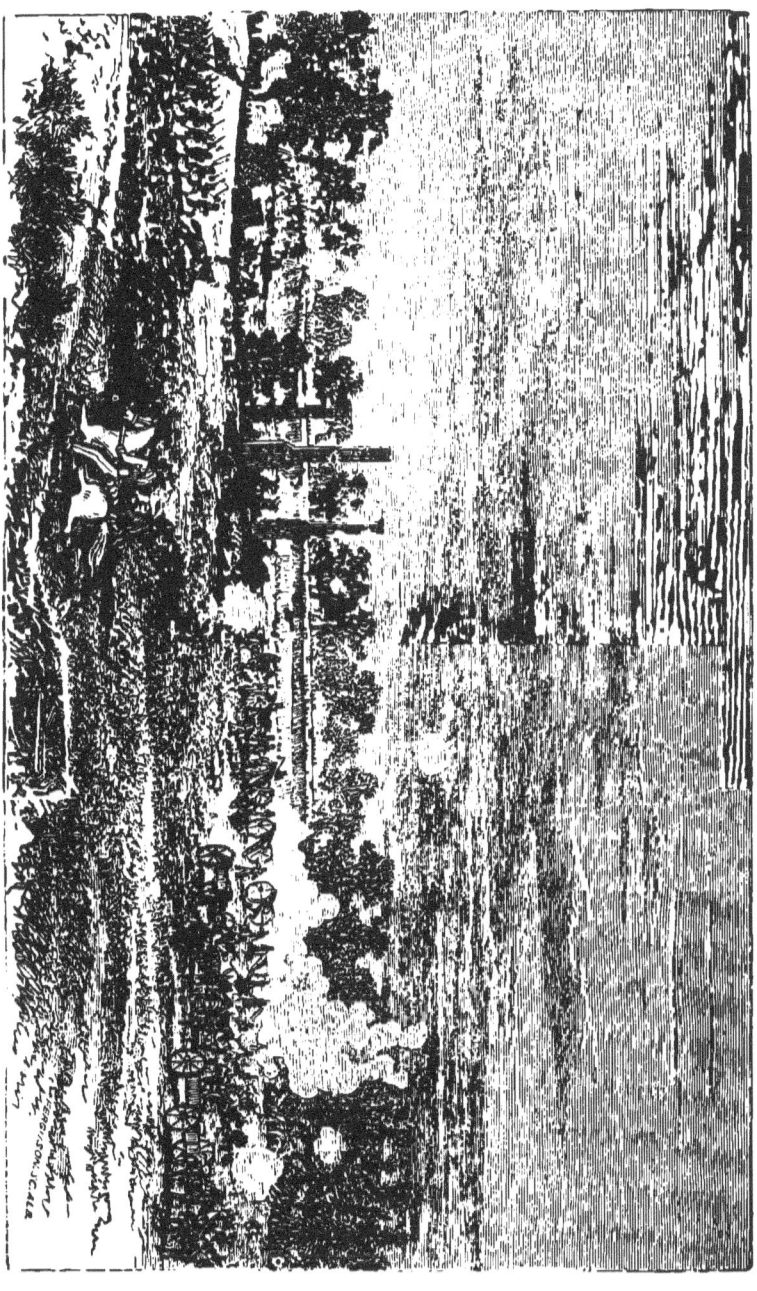

CHARGE OF THE VERMONTERS AT LEE'S MILLS.
(From "Three Years in Sixth Corps.")

creek, and made frequent attacks upon our troops at night. They were several times kept under arms through the night, expecting a general assault by the enemy. Sharpshooting and skirmishing continued almost without intermission, and men were at no time safe from rebel bullets. Rebel gunboats approached the mouth of Warwick Creek, and with their assistance the rebel infantry attempted to turn our left flank, but were repulsed and driven back.

Lee's Mills are about two miles from the James River, and six from Yorktown. On the morning of the 16th of April, 1862, the Second Division of the Sixth Corps was ordered to move, and it was understood that they were to make an assault upon the enemy's works. The troops were massed near some ruins, known as "The Chimneys," the Second, or Vermont Brigade, holding the front line, supported by the First and Third Brigades. Warwick Creek here makes up from the James River, in places narrow and deep, with abrupt banks, the land generally spreading out into marshes or swamps. On the west side were two rebel forts, with extensive rifle-pits. In front of them was an open space of some two or three hundred rods, and in the rear a dense wood, while thick wood also fringed the forts on each side. On the enemy's right the ravine through which the waters of the creek flowed expanded into a wet swamp, and the stream was so dammed up below as to flood it, thus rendering a flank movement in that direction almost impossible.

A little farther down the creek the rebels had another fort, with rifle-pits, commanding the road to Lee's Mills, which passed by these works at a distance of between two and three hundred rods. It was resolved to drive the rebels from this commanding position. At about nine o'clock in the morning, a portion of the Third Vermont, supported by Mott's Battery, advanced, as skirmishers, toward the eastern bank of the creek. The first shell they fired exploded directly over the rebel fort. With a well-manned battery of six guns our troops opened upon the rebels, with great rapidity and precision, a deadly fire of shot and shell, which was replied to with equal vigor. Their first shell exploded in front of one of our guns, killing or wounding every man but one.

An incessant fire was kept up on both sides for three hours, the marshy creek alone separating the contending forces. Soon one half the guns in the rebel forts were silenced by the fire from our batteries. The rebels then ceased to reply, and evacuated the fort. Sharpshooters were sent forward to reconnoiter, but could not ascertain what had become of the garrison. We had thus far lost seven men, and no enemy was to be seen, when our troops had three or four hours for rest.

At about four o'clock in the afternoon the rebels again appeared in possession of another breastwork, upon which they had mounted several guns. They were seen swarming through the woods in the vicinity of the fort in large numbers. Mott's Battery had been reënforced by Ayer's and Wheeler's Batteries, numbering, in all, twenty-two guns. They were brought up to within five hundred yards of the fort, to cover the charge of the Vermonters. Two companies from the Third Vermont were ordered forward, and down from the woods they came in most gallant style, rushed into the creek, where the water and mud were waist deep, and through it to the rifle-pits of the enemy, amid a shower of bullets from a long line of rifle-pits upon the opposite banks. The Vermonters pressed forward, loading and firing as they advanced. Their killed and many of their wounded sank in the stream. "But," says Abbott, in his History of the Civil War, "their comrades, instead of turning back with the wounded, seized them by the arm or the collar of the coat, and pushed resolutely on to meet the intrenched foe. As soon as they got foothold on the western bank, with a cheer, which rang like the clarion of victory, they made a dash at the enemy, concealed in the long line of rifle-pits. The rebels, in panic, fled, and sought protection behind the redoubts. The victors found, to their dismay, that many of their eartridges were soaked with water and utterly useless. Still for an hour they fought against superior numbers. The rebels were behind their ramparts. The patriots, dividing with each other the few dry cartridges they possessed, soon found their ammunition expended, while, for some unexplained reason, no reënforcements were sent to support them. Why the men should have been sent across the creek to meet a vastly outnumbering force, and then be left there to be massacred, no one has yet revealed. It is a mystery which *can*, perhaps, be explained, but unfortunately it has *not* been, and we leave it, as another of the long list of inexplicable events which have occurred during the progress of the war."

Being unsupported and out of ammunition, the brave Green Mountain Boys were forced to fall back and recross the stream under a terrible fire of the enemy. Before they could reach a place of safety, sad havoc had been made in their noble ranks. Many of the killed sank in the creek, and their bodies were never recovered. The casualties to the Vermont Brigade, in this engagement, were as follows:—

Second Regiment, 1 killed; Third Regiment, 24 killed, 7 mortally wounded, 56 wounded, 1 missing; Fourth Regiment, 3 killed, 30 wounded; Fifth Regiment, 2 killed, 6 wounded; Sixth Regiment, 11 killed, 77 wounded. Total loss to the Brigade, 218.

There were many thrilling instances of undaunted courage connected with this battle, scores of which have never been placed upon record. The Vermonters retreated in good order, carrying with them their wounded comrades. Many were shot in the water. A boy of sixteen, who was in the midst of the carnage, described the storm of lead which fell upon them by saying, " Why, sir, it was just like sap-boiling, in that stream, the bullets fell so thick."

As soon as the Vermonters reached the eastern bank, they rallied and commenced the fight again. Many of them, amidst the murderous fire of the rebels, dashed back again into the stream to help out the wounded, who were clinging to any object that presented, to save themselves. Julian A. Scott, of the Third Regiment, under sixteen years old, went back again and again, seemingly to almost certain death, and saved nine of his companions. John Harrington, but seventeen years old, having returned across the stream, through the terrific fire of the rebels, saw a wounded comrade left in one of the rifle-pits. He immediately went back and brought him away in safety. Lieutenant Whittemore watched his movements, and saved his life by shooting several rebels who were taking deliberate aim at him.

The troops were saved from almost total destruction mainly through the watchfulness and skill of Captain

Ayre, who selected just the right position for his batteries; and the moment he saw the rebels form to charge, he opened upon them from his twenty-two guns so terrible a fire that they did not dare leave their intrenchments. The fire was so accurate that every rebel cannon was silenced. One ball swept a whole file of rebels to the ground.

Private William Scott, of Co. K, Third Vermont, who, in the autumn of 1861, was found asleep at his post on the picket line, and was tried and sentenced by court martial to be shot, but was pardoned by President Lincoln, was among the mortally wounded. When his pardon was announced to him, he said, with streaming eyes, "I will show President Lincoln that I am not afraid to die for my country." He died with a prayer upon his lips for the Martyr President.

Since the battle of Lee's Mills, when General Smith's division were only waiting for an order to cross the stream and support the Vermonters, it has been ascertained that the reason why the order was not given by General McClellan, who was in command, was because he did not wish to bring on a general engagement at that time.

BATTLE OF WILLIAMSBURG.

The following account of the battle of Williamsburg, which occurred on the 5th of May, 1862, is from an officer in the Vermont Brigade: —

"Camp near Williamsburg, Va.,
May 7, 1862.

"The fight commenced at daylight, and was carried on with great vigor with musketry most of the day. General Smith's division was on the right, General Hooker's on the left, with some others on his left.

"Our brigade was not directly engaged at all, and was moved toward the right, and then to the left, wherever the commanding general deemed the rebels were gaining ground. But at near night our brigade turned the left of the enemy's line, immediately under General Smith's command, where General Sumner held us to support the left, where he feared the enemy would drive our troops.

"The rebels seemed to fight with desperation; but they were completely whipped, and had to 'skedaddle' with all possible speed.

"On our left the havoc on both sides was immense, especially in Hooker's division, which will prove to be 1500 or more killed, wounded, and missing. The loss in our brigade was 12 killed and 46 wounded, and the enemy's loss opposed to us is some 300 to 350 killed and wounded.

"We have taken a great number of prisoners, and still continue to bring them in. Our surgeons, and some of theirs, who remained, have been continually at work up to this time, and have not yet finished dressing the wounded; neither are the dead all buried.

"I think this battle will settle all doubts about General Smith, as I think that he showed himself the greatest general on the field, either old or young, and our successes ought to be credited to him and his brave troops; and we have no doubt, if he could have had his way, we should have had a more complete victory; but it is, at all events, a great one, and we are satisfied.

"Where the rebels will make another stand is more than I can tell, as they have now no strong place left. Their men, all I have seen, — which is a good many, — are the dirtiest looking human beings I have ever met. I should think six months in such condition would kill any class of men. The roads and fields are strewn with guns and equipments, and remind me of Bull Run, only it has changed sides."

BATTLE OF GOLDING'S FARM.

The general dejection that followed the retirement of our troops across the Chickahominy was particularly relieved by the good news of two considerable successes by the division of General Smith, who held a position on the extreme right, consisting of a line of breastworks and two redoubts. The left of these redoubts was strongly constructed, and had much annoyed the enemy, who had reason to believe that if heavy artillery were placed on it, they might be compelled to evacuate the high grounds at both New Bridge and Old Tavern. Indeed, it commanded these and other points.

Accordingly, when assured of the successes of the left wing of their army, the rebels determined to seize the opportunity of advancing upon Smith's redoubt. This duty was assigned to Toombs' Georgia Brigade, one of the best organizations in the Confederate service. They drove in our pickets about seven o'clock on Friday evening, June 28, and advanced, with close volleys of musketry, in two lines of battle. Hancock's Brigade, consisting of the Fifth Wisconsin, Sixth Maine, Forty-Third New York, and Forty-Ninth Pennsylvania Regiments, were immediately under arms, as indeed they had been all day, expecting to join in the contest on the other side. They advanced over a piece of corduroy road, passed the redoubt to the right, and, after traversing a bottom or declivity, formed in line of battle about a third of a mile from the redoubt, and on the ascending slope of a hill. Here they threw themselves upon their bellies, so that they could just peep over a crest by rising to their knees, and waited the onslaught of the enemy.

The pickets skirmished right into the main body, the rebels coming pell-mell after them, hoping to capture the whole force, when, just as they turned the crest of the hill, Hancock's Brigade and Brooks' Fifth Vermont Regiment gave them a staggering fire. At the same moment, the artillery from the redoubt and below opened upon them, and they fell, right and left, in heaps and files, until the desperation of the Georgians changed to doubt, and then to panic. As they attempted to fall back, our men rose to their feet, rushed some distance, and lay down again, pouring in, as before, murderous volleys. The whole fight lasted half an hour, and ended in one hundred dead Georgians being left on the field. Our loss was exceedingly slight, as our men were not only properly generaled, but the regimental officers of this brigade were some of the most effective in the service.

SECOND FIGHT OF GOLDING'S FARM.

The next morning, Saturday, the infuriated Georgians, who had, in the mean time, heard of their success of Friday across the Chickahominy, determined to attack our lines before General Smith's division a second time, and make another effort to occupy the redoubt near Golding's house. Their dead still lay in the bottom of the meadow where they had fallen the night before, and our troops had stolen around in the night to a strip of wood near a picket station, where they dug and masked a rifle-pit.

At eight o'clock the Georgians formed in line of battle, headed by Colonel Lamar, of the Seventh Georgia, known in connection with the celebrated slave case of the yacht Wanderer — the first regiment, by repute, to enter the rebel service. They did not seem dispirited by their ill success of the day before, but marched boldly up to the same inevitable fate, — terrible volleys, that cut them to pieces, literally butchering them, — and their enemy, though so obvious to feeling, was nowhere plain to the sight.

BATTLE OF SAVAGE'S STATION.

Our troops fell back leisurely to Savage's Station, and there awaited the enemy. The battle took place here on Sunday, the 29th of June, and was more sanguinary than that of the day before. It commenced about five o'clock in the afternoon, and lasted till seven o'clock at night. In the course of it, some of the sharpest infantry fighting of the war took place, in which parts of Sedgwick's, Richardson's, Hooker's, Smith's, and Kearney's forces engaged with various success. The rebels came determinedly across the field, firing as they advanced, until General Sumner ordered our troops up, at double-quick, to a charge. About four thousand of them went off at once, with a roar that might have drowned the musketry. The rebels kept their position for a moment, and then fell back to the rear of their batteries. Meagher's Brigade, however, succeeded in charging right up to the guns of a Virginia battery, two of which they had hauled off spiked, and chopped the carriages to pieces.

The Vermont Brigade had the advance of the division, and General Brooks at once threw his regiments to the front. The Fifth and Sixth as skirmishers, supported by the Third and Second in line of battle, the Fourth being thrown upon the flank, the brigade advanced rapidly through a wide strip of woods. As the line of skirmishers emerged from the woods, they suddenly received the fire of a battery and of a strong line of battle. The Fifth at once charged upon the rebels in front, who scattered in great confusion. They were beaten back, but only to re-form and press forward again from the cover of the woods to which they had retreated. Three rebel regiments advanced against the Vermont Fifth; but they had a good position, and held it in spite of the greatly superior force. The contest was a very hot one, in which the Fifth lost about two hundred of her men in killed, wounded, and missing. Many of their dead were left upon the field. The other Vermont regiments were not so hotly engaged, and their loss was comparatively small. The Confederate loss in this engagement was about four thousand.

The weary but still resolute soldiers received orders

at midnight to fall back rapidly from Savage's Station across White Oak Swamp. The enemy was making furtive attempts to overreach them in this respect, and it was likely to become a tight race between the rebels and the Unionists as to which should first cross the creek and gain the high grounds on the other side. If they should be more speedy, and succeed in placing the swamp between ourselves and them, our retreat would be almost inevitably cut off, and almost the whole army butchered or surrendered.

BATTLE OF WHITE OAK SWAMP.

Towards morning our troops crossed White Oak Creek to an elevated position, where they remained undisturbed by the enemy. They were very much exhausted by the preceding battles, and the worn-out soldiers made the most of their opportunity for rest. It did not continue long, however.

Jackson had crossed the river, and, with great secrecy, made his way to the borders of White Oak Creek, where, concealed by trees and underbrush, he had massed his batteries, and about two o'clock in the afternoon, with seventy-five pieces of artillery, opened a terrible fire upon our troops, taking them entirely by surprise. Several of Mott's caissons were blown up, and his pieces dismounted, and general confusion was created.

Very soon our light batteries recovered from the surprise, and vigorously responded to the enemy, who was soon at a perceptible disadvantage, so far as accuracy and effect were concerned. Our infantry, too, fell in line ready to support the batteries, or meet half way any attempt of the rebel infantry to push across the creek. Thus the battle progressed late in the afternoon, with serious loss on both sides — more wounds from cannon shell, perhaps, resulting than at any other time in any battle. The rebels made some desperate efforts to cross the creek, but General Smith brought his men up to close quarters with them whenever they dared the contest; and although in each case some of our best and beloved soldiers bit the dust, there were no signs of holding off. The cannon firing was incessant here, some of the deepest and closest of the war, and the infantry fire extended along whole columns.

At five o'clock they engaged the enemy, hidden by woods and the swelling of hills, and the firing from musketry and field batteries was soon intense. The rebels did fatal execution among us, and some of our most valuable officers fell here, wounded and dying. The reports of ordnance had now been heard so many days that chaos seemed the normal condition of nature, and painfully the battle went on. It was scarcely an enthusiastic fight, for all the romance of battle had worn off by reason of its monotony. The men fought well, however, though half dead with heat, thirst, and weariness. Some broke for the river, and plunged into the cool water for an instant, then emerging, rushed back to the fray, and fought like lions.

Fresh troops and superior numbers seemed bearing the tide of battle against us at five o'clock, and the fate of the army hung trembling in the sunset, when a new advocate — half of God, half of man — came to our relief.

The gunboats Galena, Aroostook, and Jacob Bell opened from Turkey Island Bend, in the James River, with shot and shell from their immense rifle guns. The previous roar of field artillery seemed as faint as the rattle of musketry in comparison with these pieces of ordnance, that literally shook the water and strained the air. Thus was the tide of battle turned in our favor.

At this stage General Heintzelman ordered a charge by his corps. The gunboats were signaled to cease their fire. Rushing steadily ahead, defying all efforts of the enemy to break or turn its line, the corps had at last the satisfaction of seeing the enemy break and fly in confusion to the swamp, totally dispirited and repulsed. We took in this engagement over two thousand prisoners.

The battle at White Oak Swamp was scarcely second to that of Gaines' Hill in point of losses of life, wounded, and prisoners. We suffered less than the enemy, who was literally butchered, but our own loss was very large. We lost all of Mott's battery but a single gun, the whole of Randall's battery, one gun of Captain Ayres', and several others in various parts of the field. Our loss in killed, wounded, and prisoners was put down at twenty-five hundred.

General Brooks was seriously wounded. His Vermont Brigade behaved like veterans in the several engagements between Gaines' Hill and White Oak Swamp. The same indomitable pluck that instigated the charge across the dam at Warwick River, marked their course in the fight of Golding's Farm, Savage's, and White Oaks. The loss of this brigade was, perhaps, less than that of any of the brigades of Smith's division.

The battle was again renewed early on Tuesday morning by the enemy, who evidently expected to crush our army. It lasted about three hours, resulting in considerable loss to both parties. The enemy then retired, leaving the field to our troops. They again advanced about three o'clock in the afternoon, in considerable force, but retired after being shelled by the gunboats and artillery for about two hours, without coming near enough for the use of musketry.

The loss of our army during these seven days' engagement is not positively known, but could not be less than twenty thousand, in killed, wounded, and missing. The loss of the enemy was very heavy, far exceeding our own.

The loss to the "Vermont Brigade" was reported as follows: —

	Killed.	Wounded.	Missing.	Total.
Second Regiment,	0	43	39	82
Third Regiment,	4	18	00	22
Fourth Regiment,	0	16	00	16
Fifth Regiment,	29	143	10	182
Sixth Regiment,	7	51	29	87
Totals,	40	271	78	389

On the Fourth of July, General McClellan issued the following proclamation to his troops: —

"*Soldiers of the Army of the Potomac:* —

"Your achievements of the past ten days have illustrated the valor and endurance of the American soldier. Attacked by superior forces, and without hopes of reënforcements, you have succeeded in changing your base of operations by a flank movement, always regarded as the most hazardous of military operations. You have saved all your guns, except a few lost in battle, taking in return guns and colors from the enemy.

"Upon your march you have been assailed, day after day, with desperate fury, by men of the same race and nation, skilfully massed and led. Under every disadvantage of number, and necessarily of position, also, you have, in every conflict, beaten back your foes with enormous slaughter.

"Your conduct ranks you among the celebrated armies of history. None will now question that each of you may always with pride say, 'I belong to the army of the Potomac.' You have reached this new base complete in organization and unimpaired in spirit. The enemy may at any time attack you; we are prepared to meet them. I have personally established your lines. Let them come, and we will convert their repulse into a final defeat. Your government is strengthening you with the resources of a great people. On this, our nation's birthday, we declare to our foes, who are rebels against the best interests of mankind, that this army shall enter the capital of the so-called Confederacy; that our national Constitution shall prevail; and that the Union, which can alone insure internal peace and external security to each State, must and shall be preserved, cost what it may, in time, treasure, and blood."

Two days before issuing this proclamation, General McClellan had given an order for the army to retreat to Harrison's Landing, six miles down the James River, as he said to be nearer his base of supplies. This order was received by many of the generals of his army with amazement, and even with indignation. They retreated from an enemy utterly broken, scattered, and panic-stricken, and when there was not a foe within miles of them. The brave Kearney said, in the presence of many officers, —

"I, Philip Kearney, an old soldier, enter my solemn protest against this order for retreat. We ought, instead of retreating, to follow up the enemy and take Richmond; and, in full view of the responsibility of such a declaration, I say to you all, such an order can only be prompted by cowardice or treason."

The army, humiliated by disaster, and yet ennobled by heroism, remained inactive, in comfortable encampment on the river banks, during the months of July and August. In the mean time the government was anxiously deliberating respecting future movements. General McClellan plead earnestly for reënforcements, that he might again march upon Richmond.

BATTLE OF CRAMPTON'S GAP.

The next engagement in which the Vermont Brigade took a part was that at Crampton's Gap, September 14, 1862. On the 5th, General Lee with his army crossed the Potomac into Maryland, and occupied Frederick City. General McClellan was ordered to push forward at once and meet him. The army left camp on the morning of the 7th, marched through

Alexandria, crossed Long Bridge to Washington, thence through Georgetown, Rockville, Johnstown, and on to Jefferson, having driven a detachment of rebels through Jefferson Pass.

The advance was sounded at ten o'clock on the morning of the 14th, and at three in the afternoon our troops were near the South Mountain range, about fifty miles from Harrison's Landing. The rebels had fallen back, taking two roads which crossed the South Mountain, through deep gorges, the northern called Turner's Pass, and the other, six miles south of it, called Crampton Pass. These passes the rebels had strongly fortified, and arranged their batteries on the crests of adjacent hills.

General Franklin approached the Crampton Pass, and when within about a mile and a half of it, formed the Sixth Corps in line of battle, while the other troops were to proceed to the South Mountain Pass, and drive the rebels through it. Between Franklin's Corps and Crampton Pass was the village of Burkettsville, beyond was the South Mountains, their summits crowned with rebel batteries and infantry, protected by heavy timber.

Late in the afternoon an attack was ordered by General Franklin's Corps, and their advance was the signal for the rebels to open fire from their well posted and protected batteries. Our troops, however, advanced steadily in the face of a storm of cannon and musket balls. After severe fighting, Slocum's troops succeeded in gaining the pass, while the Second Division pressed up the thickly wooded sides of the mountain, charging a battery at the left of the Pass, and capturing two of its guns. The Confederates fled precipitately down the west side of the mountain, and our troops were in full possession of the ground, strewed with dead rebels. The loss on our side, though large, bore no comparison with that of the rebels. The rebels made their way into Pleasant Valley, leaving on our hands their dead and wounded, three stand of colors, two pieces of artillery, and a great many prisoners.

At the South Mountain Pass, a still more desperate battle took place. With their advantage in position, it seemed almost hopeless to attempt a battle; but General Hooker brought his Corps to the assistance of the Ninth, and a terrible battle ensued, which resulted in a complete Union victory, and the possession of the ground lately occupied by the rebels. In this engagement General Reno was killed by a minie ball, which was mourned by the whole army.

While these battles were in progress another took place at Harper's Ferry, which resulted in the surrender of that place to the enemy: a severe blow to our cause, by which we lost over eleven thousand men, and a vast amount of munitions of war. The surrender of this important position has been attributed to the cowardice or treachery, or both, of Colonel Miles, a regular army officer.

BATTLE OF ANTIETAM.

Immediately following the foregoing, occurred the battle of Antietam, which took place on the seventeenth of September, 1862, where the "Vermont Brigade" also performed an important part. The following circumstantial account of this battle is given by a correspondent of the Bennington Banner: —

"As we passed through Burkettsville we were cheered on by the ladies of the place, who, for some reason unknown to me, had not been removed from the town before the battle commenced. We passed through the entire length of the village, the shot and shell from the enemy flying like Satan's angels over our heads. Skirmishers were thrown out as we neared the enemy's line, and hardly had they been deployed before they were engaged. By this time the bullets began to whistle around our heads in rather too close proximity to be safe. In consequence, General Brooks ordered us to take up our position behind a large barn which stood near us, not wishing needlessly to expose his men. As we entered the yard, one of our men was shot through the neck, and fell dead without a groan.

A few moments after, a gallant charge was made by a brigade of Slocum's division on our right, they driving the enemy before them like sheep. It was a noble sight. The time had now come; it became necessary for us to 'go in;' we filed from behind the barn, passing to the left into a smooth meadow, halted and came to front as coolly as if on drill. Next came the order to charge, and forward we went, at a double-quick, our lieutenant colonel — who is in command of the regiment — leading us a yard or two in front of the colors, which were flung out to the breeze, showing that the Stars and Stripes were once more moving onward proudly to victory. The position which we were ordered to charge upon was one of great strength, and if the enemy had held it with half the courage with which it was stormed, we should all have went under before we could have taken it; but as we gave our battle-cry they fled in every direction, hardly waiting to fire a shot. We halted a moment as we came to the stone wall bounding the field across which we had charged; but not long after, the order came to move on, and onward we moved, over the wall, through the woods, up the mountain sides, sweeping with irresistible fury every thing before us. The top of the mountain was gained, and every man was thankful that he was alive, and realizing that it was indeed a miracle that one of us was left to tell the tale. We halted a moment to take breath, and then started along the ridge of the mountain, determined to take a battery which had been throwing all kinds of deadly missiles at us during our charge. Our progress was necessarily very slow, being through tangled brush and over rocks, equal to any found on the Green Mountains. Onward we went, however, deterred by nothing that obstructed our route; yet the rebels got the start of us, and had their battery removed before we reached the spot where it was posted.

"In our charge we captured the battle-flag of the ninteenth Virginia, one major, three lieutenants, and sixty prisoners. I am unable to give you a list of them, owing to the hurry in which they were sent to the rear, their names not being taken at brigade headquarters. The major and lieutenants were from the sixteenth Virginia, as were also the greater part of the prisoners. The major states that we utterly annihilated the sixteenth, and that now it is classed among the things that were. The Vermont Brigade also captured twenty-eight other prisoners from the fifteenth North Carolina, twenty-fourth Georgia, seventh Virginia cavalry, sixth Virginia infantry, tenth Georgia, Cobb's first Georgia Legion, and a lieutenant from the Troop artillery.

"This was one of the most hardly-contested and terrific battles of the entire war. Half the officers of the thirty-fourth New York were disabled, their colors were shot to pieces, every one of their color-guard wounded, and but a handful of men left. Only thirty-four of the whole regiment could be brought together after the fight. The fifteenth Massachusetts went into the battle with seventeen officers and six hundred men. They came out with nine officers and one hundred and thirty-four men. All the efforts of Howard and Sumner were unavailing to reorganize the troops, or to check the impetuous advance of the foe. Our troops were withdrawn to the rear, and again the trampled cornfield, strewn with our dead and dying, was in the hands of the rebels. Their farther advance was, however, checked by the well-directed fire of our artillery.

"It was one o'clock. The prospect looked gloomy. Hooker was carried from the field wounded; his Corps greatly exhausted; the ammunition of several of the batteries was expended, and they had been compelled to retire. All that had been gained had been lost. We could now only hope to hold our own. Advance was impossible. At this crisis Franklin appeared with fresh troops, and formed sublimely on the left. General Smith, with his Maine and Vermont troops, was ordered to retake the cornfield. Magnificently it was done. His troops, on the double-quick, swept the field like a cloud-shadow, penetrated the forest, and in ten minutes had gained them both. So sudden are the changes in the kaleidoscope of battle! Now for a couple of hours there was a slight lull in this tempest of death, though the thunders of artillery were incessantly echoing over the hills.

"The battle continued until night, when it ceased, and it was supposed would be resumed next morning. Toward morning it was known that the rebels were moving back. Next day the rebels buried their dead under a truce, during which they were making preparations for their escape. On the night of the 18th the whole rebel army disappeared. Thus ended one of the most sanguinary and bloody battles of the war."

BATTLE OF FREDERICKSBURG.

The battle of Fredericksburg occurred on the 13th of December, 1862. Between the time of the battle of Antietam and that of Fredericksburg, General McClellan was relieved of the command of the Army of the Potomac, and was succeeded by Major General A. E. Burnside. General Brooks, who had commanded the "Vermont Brigade" through many hard-fought battles, was assigned to the command of the Sixth Division, to succeed General Slocum, who took command of the Twelfth Corps. General Brooks, though of abrupt and stern manners, was one of the bravest and most energetic brigade commanders in the army, and had greatly endeared himself to his brigade. On surrendering the command, he was presented by the officers of the "Vermont Brigade" with a magnificent silver service. It is said that, forgetting his rough manners, he received the beautiful gift of his loved brigade with tears standing on his brown cheeks. He was succeeded in the command of the brigade by Colonel Henry Whiting, of the Second Vermont Regiment.

The army remained comparatively inactive from the last of September until November, when it moved to the Rappahannock, opposite Fredericksburg, formerly the most important town in Spottsylvania County, Virginia. It is on the south bank of the Rappahannock River, at the head of tide-water, about sixty miles north of Richmond, and in connection with it both by railroad and turnpike road. It had been a very prosperous town; but some years before the breaking out of the rebellion the tide of its success had been receding, so that in 1861 it had a population of only about four thousand.

General Burnside's plan was to cross the Rappahannock by forced marches, and so on to Richmond before General Lee could concentrate his army so as successfully to oppose him. On arrival at Falmouth it was found that the pontoon bridges, which were to have been sent from Washington, had not arrived. The delay in their arrival, and the time required to put them across the river, annoyed as our men were, day and night, by the fire of the enemy on the opposite side of the river, gave ample time to bring the rebel army together at Fredericksburg, and strongly to fortify themselves for a defense, and to dispute the crossing of our troops at any point for twenty miles up and down the river. The rebel army was so distributed that General Burnside believed that by throwing his whole army across the river at one point he could break through the extended line of the enemy before a sufficient force could be concentrated to successfully oppose his movements. After throwing his forces across the river, one of the severest battles of the war took place, resulting in no victory to either army, though the loss on our side was much the greatest in killed and wounded, the enemy having greatly the advantage in position. Our army returned across the river during the night of the 13th, in good order, without the loss of a man or a gun.

In this battle the "Vermont Brigade," under command of Colonel Henry Whiting, behaved well, as usual, and was distinguished for its bravery and coolness throughout the fight. The casualties in the brigade were as follows:—

Second Regiment, killed, 2; wounded, 59. Third Regiment, killed, 2; wounded, 8. Fourth Regiment, killed, 11; wounded 43; missing, 2. Fifth Regiment, killed, 10; wounded, 30. Sixth Regiment, killed 1; wounded, 1. Totals, killed, 26; wounded, 141; missing, 2.

General Burnside, in his preliminary report of this engagement to President Lincoln, said, "For the failure of the attack, I am responsible, as the extreme gallantry, courage, and endurance showed by them (the patriotic soldiers) was never excelled, and would have carried the point had it been possible. But for the fog, and the unexpected and unavoidable delay in building the bridges, which gave the enemy twenty-four hours more to concentrate his forces in his strong positions, we should almost certainly have succeeded."

SECOND BATTLE OF FREDERICKSBURG.

The second battle of Fredericksburg occurred on the 3d and 4th of May, 1863. Colonel Whiting having resigned, the "Vermont Brigade" was commanded by Colonel L. A. Grant, of the Fifth Regiment. Adjutant General Washburn, in his annual report to the Legislature in 1863, says, "The coolness and bravery with which the brigade fought at the second battle of Fredericksburg, on the 3d of May, and at Banks' Ford on the 4th of May, have never been excelled by any troops. They stormed and carried the heights of Fredericksburg on the 3d of May, in the face of a terrific fire ; and when, on the 4th, they protected the rear of the Sixth Corps, and enabled it to cross the Rappahannock in safety, the masses of the enemy, greatly outnumbering them, was persistently hurled against them in vain. They were attacked by, and repulsed three rebel brigades, of four regiments each, and saved the Sixth Corps. The following is Colonel Grant's report, dated May 4, 1863 : —

"*Peter T. Washburn, Adjutant and Inspector General:*

"Sir: I have the honor to report the most brilliant conduct of the Vermont troops at the storming of the heights of Fredericksburg yesterday. The Second Vermont was the first regiment in the principal works on the highest range of hills, and the Sixth Vermont was the second regiment in the works on the lower range of hills commanding Fredericksburg.

"The heights were carried by storm, at the point of the bayonet, under a terrific fire from the enemy. The Second Vermont led the charge, and covered itself with glory. It could not have been done better.

"Colonel Walbridge and Major Tyler are deserving of special praise for the great coolness and gallantry displayed on the occasion.

"The Sixth Regiment, Colonel Barney, did splendidly. The Third Regiment, Colonel Seaver, the

Fourth Regiment, Colonel Stoughton, and the Fifth Regiment, Lieutenant Colonel Lewis, constituted a reserve force, and came to the support of the advance in splendid style.

"Three pieces of artillery and many prisoners were taken. Further particulars shall be given. The Second lost 12 killed and 94 wounded; the Third lost 1 killed and 6 wounded; the Fourth lost 1 wounded; the Fifth none; the Sixth lost 8 wounded. Total, 122."

The following is a portion of Colonel Grant's report in regard to the second day's engagement: —

"*Peter T. Washburn, Adjutant and Inspector General:*

"SIR: The First Vermont Brigade has again met the enemy, and done honor to the State.

"After the storming of the heights of Fredericksburg, on the 3d instant, we were ordered forward upon the plank road to join the main army. About three miles from Fredericksburg the advance met, and became hotly engaged with reënforcements marching to the support of the force just driven from the heights.

"The Vermont Brigade arrived in the midst of the battle, and was immediately ordered to take position on the left, to repel any flank attack in that direction. With skirmishers well in front, four regiments of the brigade were deployed in line, the Second Vermont being held in reserve. In that position we remained during the night.

"In the morning it was found that other reënforcements had come up from the left, taken possession of the heights, and passed to our rear, completely cutting us off from Fredericksburg. We immediately changed direction to the rear, facing toward Fredericksburg.

"The disposition of troops at this time was as follows: There was one brigade in our front, a large portion of which was deployed upon the skirmish line, which occupied a crest overlooking a ravine between us and the rebel forces. Just in the rear of the brigade thus deployed was another small ravine, in which was a thin skirt of woods. Just in the rear of this ravine, behind a crest or slight swell of ground, the Vermont Brigade took its position, and constituted a second and strong line of defense. The Fifth Vermont, Lieutenant Colonel Lewis, was posted on the extreme right, and considerably in front, to support a section of artillery. That position being to the right of the brigade in our front, two companies were thrown out as skirmishers. The Third Vermont, Colonel Seaver, was on the right of the main line, and the Sixth Vermont, Colonel Barney, was on the left of the Third. Between the Third and the Sixth was a battery. The Second Vermont, Colonel Walbridge, occupied the left of the Sixth, and the Twenty-sixth New Jersey, Lieutenant Colonel Martindale, was on the left of the Second. The Fourth Vermont, Colonel Stoughton, was posted on the extreme left, and considerably to the front, in the edge of the thick pine woods, in position commanding a ravine and open space in front. In this position we awaited the attack.

"The attack commenced a few minutes past five, P. M., upon General Brooks' skirmishers at our right. This proved a feint, as the main attack was soon made in strong force directly upon our front. Long lines of rebel infantry, one after another, charged down the slope into the ravine in front of our pickets. One rebel battery after another unmasked and opened fire. The left of the main attack bore directly down toward the Fifth Vermont, and its skirmishers retired, fighting inch by inch.

"The pickets or skirmishers of the other brigade were driven in. As soon, however, as the enemy's lines had gained the crest from which the pickets had been driven, they bore to the left to gain the woods, and to separate us from the river. The section of artillery, near the Fifth Vermont, retired, having exhausted their ammunition.

"Lieutenant Colonel Lewis immediately threw forward the right of his regiment upon the crest, and poured into the advancing lines a terrible cross and enfilading fire, causing great havoc in their ranks. Still they went on, yelling like demons. The Fifth Vermont continued its fire, with great rapidity, upon their flank and rear, until another column, further to the right, came bearing down to the rear of the Fifth, threatening to cut it off. Seeing this, Lieutenant Colonel Lewis, agreeably to previous instructions, drew off his regiment by the flank, passing round, through a depression, to the right of the Third Vermont.

"While this was being done, and the lines in our front were giving away, the Twenty-Sixth New Jersey was ordered to the front and right, and the Second Vermont was moved to the left, so as to occupy the place left by the Twenty-Sixth. The Third Vermont was also moved up to take the former position of the Second, thus leaving the Sixth Vermont and the battery on the right. The Twenty-Sixth broke and gave way, and the enemy gained the woods in front of the Second, and were advancing directly upon them, when the Second rose, and poured upon them a well-directed fire, and continued it with such rapidity as to resemble volley immediately upon volley. The Twenty-Sixth passed away from the front, so that the Third opened, and, with the Second, poured its leaden hail full upon the already confused masses of the advancing hosts. The enemy were here checked, broken, and held at bay. Still further to the left, as the enemy advanced, the Fourth Vermont became engaged. As the enemy advanced obliquely, the Fourth would have been exposed to a cross fire, but Colonel Stoughton, with great coolness, threw back his right wing, presenting a bold front, and poured into them a terrible fire. Still on they went, gaining the ravine in front of the Fourth; and at the same time a force further to the left came up, driving in our front lines, threatening to cut us off from the river.

"Colonel Stoughton now changed front forward to his original position, and poured in fresh volleys, holding the enemy's lines in check. In the meantime the Fifth Vermont had arrived from the right, and been posted behind a crest, to support the Second.

"Seeing that Colonels Walbridge and Seaver were able to hold their front, and that the enemy were pressing to turn our left, I ordered the Fifth further to the left, and to a position completely commanding the ravine, should the enemy succeed in flanking the Fourth. At this time the roar of battle was terrible. The roar of cannon and the rattle of musketry surpassed all description. The enemy had three times our number in front; but the Vermont regiments stood firm and unbroken, hugging closely to the crest, and literally presenting a wall of fire. Baffled in their efforts to break through our lines, and perceiving that the battery on our right had left its position, the enemy rallied, and made an attempt to turn our right; but the Sixth Vermont were there.

"The rebels, not knowing what awaited them, rushed desperately forward, and nearly gained the crest, when the Sixth rose, and poured a terrible volley into their quivering ranks, and then immediately charged upon them, down the slope, through the ravine, on to the crest in front, from which our front line had been driven. In the meantime Lieutenant Colonel Martindale had rallied the Twenty-Sixth, and charged down with the Sixth.

"The enemy were utterly routed. They gave way in great confusion, and many of them were taken prisoners. The ground in front of the Second, Third, and Sixth was literally covered with the rebel dead and wounded. So far as this point was concerned, a complete victory was gained; but on the left the enemy was still pressing to cut us off from the river.

"I ordered the Second, Third, and Sixth Vermont, and the Twenty-sixth New Jersey from the positions they held, and the ground they had so nobly won, to form a new line to the left, and nearer the river. Not knowing what danger was on the left, and being conscious of having gained a splendid victory, the colonels commanding these regiments at first questioned the authenticity of the order; but being informed that the order was imperative, they quickly changed position as directed. At this point of time the enemy was making a desperate attempt to force our left. He had gained the woods to the left of the Fourth and Fifth, and fearing for the safety of the Fourth, which was now almost unsupported, I withdrew that regiment, and it was placed in support of Butler's Battery, from Newton's Division, whose timely arrival and deadly fire assisted in checking the enemy's advance at that point. Darkness now came on, and the battle ceased, the enemy having been completely foiled in his attempt by the remarkable coolness and brilliant conduct of the Vermont troops.

"Not knowing the strength of the force between our left and the river, I formed a new line in a strong position, prepared to repel any attack. The regiments in this new line were formed from left to right, in the following order, to wit, the Fifth, Sixth, Twenty-sixth, Third, Second, and Fourth. The Fifth was deployed as skirmishers, its left resting on the river. In this position the brigade held the front, while the balance of the corps fell back to Banks' Ford, where bridges had been constructed to cross the river. The brigade then slowly retired, its skirmishers following in the rear. Upon arriving near the Ford, the brigade formed a new line of battle, and sent skirmishers far to the front (which had now become our rear).

"The skirmish line being attacked, the Second, Third, and Sixth Vermont regiments were sent out to support the skirmish line. The balance of the corps crossed the river, then these regiments and the skirmish line followed. To Colonel T. O. Seaver, Third Vermont, acting as general officer of the day, is due the credit of bringing off these three regiments. To Major C. P Dudley, Fifth Vermont, under the direction of Colonel Seaver, is due the credit of safely bringing off the skirmish line, the last squads crossing the river in boats, after the bridges were partially removed.

"So far as space will admit, this is a faithful account of the part taken by the Vermont troops in the battle of Banks' Ford. It was a terrible struggle. If we believe what intelligent prisoners informed us, the rebel General Lee was present, directing the attack. He skillfully massed and hurled against us a terrible force, fully expecting to annihilate or capture the whole corps. No less than three corps of the rebel army were engaged, and no less than three brigades fought the 'Green Mountain Boys,' to wit, a Louisiana, a North Carolina, and a Mississippi brigade, each consisting of four regiments.

"The Louisiana and North Carolina brigades must have been nearly annihilated. The colonel commanding the Louisiana brigade, whom we captured, admitted that we had taken, and killed and wounded, the most of his brigade. The number of prisoners actually captured must have been over one thousand, but owing to the imperative order withdrawing the Second, Third, and Sixth Vermont, and Twenty-sixth New Jersey, only about four hundred were brought away, among whom were one brigadier-general, one colonel, commanding brigade, several lieutenant colonels, majors, and line officers.

"Too much praise cannot be awarded to the officers and men for their excellent conduct. They could not have done better. Vermont may well be proud of them all. The men did their duty, and the officers were there to direct and encourage. Not an officer failed to come to time. Not a man straggled from the ranks. And when a regiment moved, it did it with almost the precision of an ordinary drill. It would be impossible, and almost invidious, to particularize, but I cannot fail to speak in the highest terms of praise of Colonel Walbridge, Second Vermont, Colonel Seaver, Third Vermont, Colonel Stoughton, Fourth Vermont, Colonel Barney, Sixth, and Lieut. Colonel Lewis, of the Fifth Vermont. Nor can I fail to mention in the same strain, of gallant services performed by the officers of my staff, Captain A. Brown, Fourth Vermont Volunteers, Acting Assistant Inspector General; Lieutenant C. H. Forbes, Fifth Vermont Volunteers, Acting

Assistant Adjutant General; Lieutenant J. J. Bain, Second Vermont, and F. J. Butterfield, Sixth Vermont, Acting Aids-de-Camp, and Lieutenant Horace French, Third Vermont, Acting Provost Marshal, all of whom rendered the most efficient aid. They were everywhere in the thickest of the fight, wherever needed, faithfully delivering and carrying out my orders. This was also true of them at the battle of Fredericksburg.

"Lieutenant A. Austin, Fifth Vermont Volunteers, Acting Quartermaster of the Brigade, is also entitled to great credit for supplying the command with rations and other necessaries, and for safely keeping charge of the baggage of the brigade.

"Nor ought I to fail to speak of the gallant dead. Captain Ainsworth, of the Sixth Vermont, fell while gallantly leading on his men.

"The loss to the Vermont troops was, considering all the circumstances, very slight indeed. There were 17 killed, 118 wounded, and 44 missing, in all 179. The loss inflicted upon the enemy was probably five times that number. Let not the mothers, wives, and sisters of Vermont weep for the fallen. Their graves are on the fields of battle, while their spirits find 'congenial joys in the fields of the blessed.'"

The "Vermont Brigade" was again engaged at Fredericksburg on the 5th of June, 1863. The fol-

GEN. LEWIS A. GRANT.

lowing is Colonel L. A. Grant's report to Adjutant General P. T. Washburn, dated the 6th:—

"SIR: The Vermont Brigade has again crossed the Rappahannock at the old point, about one and a half miles below Fredericksburg. It is the first brigade across, and so far as my knowledge extends, it is the only one yet over.

"We left camp yesterday, soon after noon, and marched to the river, a distance of about five miles. The pontoons were on the ground, ready to be taken down the bank and thrown across the river. The rebels had constructed rifle-pits in front of, and commanding the point where the bridges were to be placed. These rifle-pits were occupied by rebel infantry. As soon as the artillery could be got into position, it opened a terrible fire upon the rifle-pits. It had but little effect, however, except to keep back reenforcements that were coming to the assistance of those already in the rifle-pits. But very few of those in the rifle-pits were injured by the artillery fire. They managed to keep up a galling musketry fire upon the engineers that attempted to construct the bridges. It was determined to drive the rebels from the rifle-pits. The Fifth Vermont, Lieut. Colonel Lewis, and Twenty sixth New Jersey, Lieut. Colonel Martindale, were ordered forward for that purpose. They rushed gallantly down the bank, and, with the assistance of the engineers, and under a galling fire from the rifle-pits, they launched the pontoon boats into the stream, jumped into them, and rowed across and landed upon the south bank.

"But a few companies of the Fifth had crossed, when they sprang upon the bank, and with shouts charged the rifle-pits, driving the enemy from them in great confusion, taking many of them prisoners. The Twenty-sixth New Jersey came gallantly to the support of the Fifth, and did well, but it is believed that the Fifth cleared the rifle-pits. The Third Vermont, Colonel Seaver, the Fourth Vermont, Colonel Stoughton, and the Second Vermont, Colonel Walbridge, also crossed in boats, and gallantly supported the regiments already across.

"The rebels were driven across the plain into the woods. One bridge was soon completed, and the Sixth Vermont, Colonel Barney, also crossed. Our positions were taken, and are still held.

"It is impossible, at this time, to give particular instances of dashing gallantry, though there were many. It was quick work, and splendidly executed. The number of prisoners taken is not at this time known, but it is believed to be between one and two hundred. Captain Davenport sent in two officers and thirty-four enlisted men, who surrendered to him after dark, and over Deep Creek, where Captain Davenport, of the Fifth, and Captain Benton, of the Fourth, had been sent on picket.

"The casualties in the Fifth Vermont are seven wounded. No casualties in either of the other Vermont regiments."

On the 8th of June Colonel Grant further reports to General Washburn, and says: —

"It was an exciting and brilliant affair, and no account can do ample justice to the brave officers and men engaged. Impetuous enthusiasm, when displayed in the face of the enemy, beggars description. The two companies first in the works were the Rutland Company, Captain B. R. Jenne, Fifth, and the Swanton Company, Captain Friend H. Barney, Fifth. The first man in the rifle-pits was private Henry Moren, Company G.

"On Saturday, the 6th, the Sixth Vermont was skirmishing nearly all day. They occupied a position from the river on the left, by the Bernard House, round across the Bowling Green road to Deep Creek. The Sixth lost in the skirmish of that day four killed and thirteen wounded. Among the wounded was Lieutenant Raistrick. There were no casualties in the Second, Third, and Fourth Regiments. The loss of the Fifth and Sixth Regiments was four killed and twenty wounded. The loss of the Twenty-sixth New

Jersey Regiment was two killed and seventeen wounded, making a total loss of forty-three in the brigade.

"The brigade was the only force upon the south side of the river for nearly twenty-four hours. On the afternoon of the 6th another brigade came over to our support, and on the morning of the 7th we were relieved from the skirmish line, but continued to hold the front line of battle until the evening of the 7th, when we were relieved by another division, and marched back to the north side of the river, having held the front, in face of the enemy, about fifty hours. During a portion of the time the enemy developed a very large force in our front. Officers and men behaved as become Vermonters during the entire action."

BATTLE OF GETTYSBURG.

Under date of July 11, 1863, Colonel Grant, commanding "Vermont Brigade," reports to Adjutant General Washburn, that "this brigade was not hotly engaged at the battle of Gettysburg. We arrived on the battle-field at about five o'clock, P. M., of the second day's battle, having marched thirty miles that day. The position taken by the brigade was on the extreme left of the army, where it was held in reserve and to guard against any flank attack. On the

4th instant the Fourth Regiment was sent forward to feel of the enemy's right, and quite a smart skirmish followed, in which our men showed their usual gallantry. Our loss was one man, John F. Marshall, wounded in the arm and knee severely.

"Yesterday, the 10th instant, at an early hour, we advanced from Boonsboro', on the Hagerstown pike. The brigade had the advance of the infantry force, but General Buford's cavalry was in advance of this brigade. The enemy was met about three miles from Boonsboro', and driven by the cavalry about three miles, to near Funkstown. Here the cavalry met the enemy's infantry, and, after skirmishing a while, fell back, leaving the brigade in front. At the time the cavalry fell back, this brigade was about one and a half miles in advance of any support except one battery.

"The enemy, seeing the cavalry fall back, immediately advanced their skirmishers to gain a crest and some woods previously occupied by our cavalry; but the Fifth and Sixth Regiments immediately advanced their skirmishers, and took possession of the woods and crest before the enemy could do so. The enemy then opened a terrible artillery fire upon our skirmish line and the woods, and continued it for several minutes, from batteries near Funkstown, beyond the range of our artillery.

"It was evident at a glance that the position was an important one, and that the enemy would be likely to follow up their artillery fire by an infantry attack. To repel this, Colonel Stoughton, of the Fourth, was sent to support the Fifth, and Colonel Seaver, of the Third, was sent to support the Sixth, and the Second, Colonel Walbridge, was brought forward to support the battery. Colonels Stoughton and Seaver had instructions to deploy so much of their respective regiments as might be found necessary to hold the line at all hazards. Their arrival was opportune, for the enemy not only threw forward his skirmishers, but advanced strong lines of infantry, and charged upon our skirmish line. The advance was nobly met and severely repulsed. A considerable portion of the Fourth, and three companies of the Third, were deployed, to strengthen such portions of the line of the Fifth and Sixth as were attacked by the enemy's main force. The enemy repeatedly charged upon our line, and were as often met and driven back.

" While this was going on in the front, it was found that the enemy had advanced a force to our left, and were crossing the Antietam, to get in the rear of the left of our skirmish line. Colonel Walbridge was immediately dispatched, with five companies of the Second, to repel their advance and drive them back, which was most effectually done. At this point of time the brigade was nearly all employed upon the skirmish line, which extended a distance of two or three miles, with no support within one and a half miles, except the three companies of the Second, which were left in support of the battery.

"It is believed that another instance of a skirmish line, necessarily extending over so great a distance, repeatedly repelling the assaults of strong lines of infantry at different points, cannot be found in the history of any war. It is said that as the enemy's lines went back in confusion, some of our men jumped upon a fence, and, tauntingly calling them cowards, told them to come back; that there was nothing there but militia.

"Our loss was nine killed and fifty-nine wounded, in all sixty-eight. The enemy's loss could not have been less than two hundred or three hundred, for at every point they were terribly slaughtered. Among our wounded, I regret to name such gallant officers as Colonel Stoughton, of the Fourth Vermont, Lieutenant Drury, of the Second Vermont, Lieutenant Martin, of the Fourth Vermont, and Lieutenant Kimball, of the Sixth Vermont."

BATTLE OF RAPPAHANNOCK STATION.

Our army met the enemy in force at Rappahannock Station, on the 7th of November, 1863. The Vermont

Brigade was not act vely engaged, but was under a heavy artillery fire all the afternoon, without casualties.

On the 8th of November the brigade crossed the Rappahannock, and went into camp near Brandy Station. On the 27th they moved about four miles, in support of the Third Corps at the battle of Locust Grove. The brigade was not engaged, but was under heavy artillery fire, causing a few casualties.

On the 28th of November they joined the right of the main army at Robertson's Tavern, and were in line of battle on the east bank of Mine River until December 2d, when they re-crossed the Rapidan, and again went into camp near Brandy Station, where they remained most of the time inactive, until the 4th of May, 1864, when they crossed the Rapidan at Germania Ford, and went into camp two miles south of it.

BATTLES OF THE WILDERNESS.

On the 12th of March, 1864, General U. S. Grant was appointed Lieutenant General, and constituted Commander-in-Chief of all the armies of the United States. President Lincoln is said to have asked General Grant what was next to be done, and he replied, "Destroy Lee's army, and take Richmond."

The battles of the Wilderness took place from the 5th to the 10th of May, 1864, and were among the most sanguinary of the war. The "Vermont Brigade" was engaged in most of them, and suffered severely in killed, wounded, and missing. Colonel Lewis A. Grant was promoted to brigadier general on the 27th of April, 1864, and was in command of the brigade. The following concise account of the participation of this brigade in those engagements, is from Adjutant General Washburn's report for 1864: —

"On the 4th of May the Brigade crossed the Rapidan at Germania Ford, and encamped for the night two miles south of the Ford. The next two days they were engaged in the battle of the Wilderness, one of the most important and sanguinary of the war. On the morning of the 5th they were moved up the Brock road, across the old pike to where the Brock road crosses the plank road. The rebels were moving, in heavy columns, down the old pike and the plank road, which run nearly parallel from Orange Court House to Chancellorsville, about two miles apart, and in the general direction of the river — intending to pierce the Union lines, and sever from the main army Hancock's Corps, which had crossed the river at a ford below the Germania Ford, and was coming into position from the direction of Chancellorsville, upon the Brock road, beyond the point where that road crosses the plank road. The Vermont Brigade, and two other brigades of the same division, — the First and Fourth, — were detached for this occasion from the Sixth

Corps. As the brigade came to the place where the roads crossed, they found the rebel advance driving before them the Union cavalry down the plank road, and within a short distance of the crossing, which was the key of the position. Here the brigade was formed, and hastily threw up slight intrenchments upon the right of the road and in its direction. They were then ordered to advance and attack, and it would seem that the enemy were advancing to attack at the same time. The two lines met in the compact woods, where neither could see the other at any distance, and the sanguinary battle of the Wilderness commenced. Probably no more fearfully destructive fire of musketry was ever maintained. The rebels had the advantage of being protected by a slight swell of ground, and rained their showers of bullets upon the unprotected ranks of the 'Old Brigade.' And their fire was unflinchingly met and returned. Officers of rank and men were falling every moment; the ranks were becoming fearfully thinned, but no man thought of retreating. They held the very key of the position of the whole army. If they faltered, Hancock's Corps, which was then coming into position upon their left, would be cut off from the residue of the army, and perhaps be destroyed by the simultaneous attack, on front and flank, of overwhelming masses of the enemy. But the brave men of Vermont held their position, and repulsed gloriously every attempt to dislodge them, and notwithstanding every regimental commander in the brigade, except one, was either killed or wounded. They slept that night amid the horrors of the battle-field, with the dead bodies of their comrades about them, and the groans of the wounded and dying filling the air. One thousand brave officers and men of the Vermont Brigade fell on that bloody field.

"On the morning of the 6th, the brigade again advanced to the attack, moving up the plank road, with four lines of battle in their front. The enemy had fallen back, but were met about a mile from the cross roads, and the fierce conflict again commenced. The brigade occupied a slightly elevated position, where the enemy had thrown together two irregular lines of old logs and decayed timber. The four lines in front of them were swept away by the tide of battle, and the advancing enemy came upon the 'Vermont Brigade' with great force, but were checked by the fierce fire that met them, and thrown back in confusion. Again and again they advanced to the attack, and were as often repulsed, until the Union forces upon the right and left had given way or fallen back. Then the enemy closed round upon the left and rear, and at the same time again attacked in front. The position was most critical; but the brave old brigade remained sufficiently long to signally repulse the attack in front, and then, taking advantage of the confusion caused in the rebel ranks, fell back safely to the intrenchments which they had constructed upon the Brock road. Here, again, late in the afternoon, the enemy made another vigorous, determined, and desperate attack, but were driven back, repulsed, and defeated.

"On the morning of the 7th, a strong skirmish line was sent out, under command of Major Crandall, of the Sixth Regiment, who was entirely successful, driving back the enemy's skirmishers sufficiently to ascertain that their main body had retired, and capturing a large number of muskets, which the enemy had collected from the battle-field of the previous days. In the afternoon the brigade joined the Sixth Corps, and soon after dark commenced the flank movement toward Spottsylvania.

"The brigade crossed the Rapidan on the 4th of May, with about twenty-eight hundred effective men. The losses in the battles of the Wilderness, May 5th and 6th, were twelve hundred and thirty-two, as follows: —

	Killed.	Wounded.	Missing.	Total.
Brigade Staff,	0	1	1	2
Second Regiment,	45	220	32	297
Third Regiment,	34	184	21	239
Fourth Regiment,	39	189	29	257
Fifth Regiment,	28	179	31	238
Sixth Regiment,	30	152	17	199
Totals,	176	925	131	1232

"The unusual proportion of casualties is the best evidence both of the severity of the fight and the bravery of the officers and men engaged.

"The casualties among the officers were particularly severe. Of the Second Regiment, Colonel Newton Stone, Lieutenant Colonel John S. Tyler, and Captain Orville Bixby; of the Third Regiment, Captain Enoch H. Bartlett, Captain Erastus Buck, and Adjutant Abel Morrill; of the Fourth Regiment, Captain Daniel W Farr, Captain Daniel Lillie, and Lieutenants Isaac A. Putnam, Thomas Ensworth, Winfield S. Wooster, and William H. Martin; of the Fifth Regiment, Captains Alonzo R. Hurlburt, George D. Davenport, and Charles J. Ormsbee, and Lieutenants Orvis H. Sweet and Watson O. Beach; and of the Sixth Regiment, Colonel Elisha L. Barney, and Captains Riley A. Bird and George C. Randall, and Lieutenant Albert A. Crane, were either killed or died of the wounds received. They were of Vermont's bravest sons, and such as she could ill afford to spare. Colonel George P. Foster, of the Fourth Regiment, and Lieutenant Colonel John R. Lewis, commanding Fifth Regiment, were both severely wounded."

On the 5th of May the brigade marched for Chancellorsville, and arrived there on the morning of the 8th. On the morning of the 9th, the Fourth Regiment, under command of Major Pratt, was sent out to skirmish with the enemy in front, and the residue of the brigade fortified their position under a fire of artillery and musketry at long range. The Fourth Regiment lost several men upon the skirmish line.

On the 10th of May the Fourth Regiment drove the enemy's skirmishers back to their line of works, behaving with great coolness and courage, and received high commendation.

The Second Regiment, under command of Lieutenant Colonel S. E. Pingree, the Fifth, Major C. P. Dudley, the Sixth, Colonel O. A. Hale, the whole under command of Colonel Thomas O. Seaver, of the Third Regiment, composed a part of the column commanded by Colonel Upton, which charged the enemy's works. The charging column was disposed in three lines, the Vermont regiments forming the rear lines. Says Adjutant General Washburn, in his annual report for 1864, "The front lines were at first successful, capturing the works and many prisoners, but were driven back by the enemy. The three Vermont regiments, under Colonel Seaver, then advanced, and under a most galling fire, occupied the rebel works, while the other regiments fell back. Orders were given for all to fall back; but they failed to reach the Second Regiment and some of each of the others, who remained in the works, obstinately defending them against all attacks of the enemy, and refusing to fall back, protesting that they could hold the works for six months, if supplied with rations and ammunition, until they received positive orders to do so. In this charge, the gallant Major Dudley, of the Fifth Regiment, fell of wounds, of which he subsequently died. His loss was severely felt in the brigade and at home. The four companies of the Third Regiment, on the skirmish line, advanced with the attacking column, and a portion of them remained in the rebel works until the last."

On the 11th of May the brigade held its position, and was constantly under fire, and on the morning of the 12th moved with the Corps to the left, to coöperate with the Second Corps, under General Hancock, who had made his celebrated charge, capturing two general officers, several guns, and many prisoners, and was vigorously defending the works he had captured against a superior force of the enemy The brigade marched into position under a terrific fire from the rebel batteries, and lost a number of men. The brigade was formed in two lines on the extreme left. Brigadier General Grant, with the regiments of the second line, was ordered to the right, to assist General Wheaton, and Colonel Seaver was left in command of the front line. General Wheaton was endeavoring to advance with his brigade, in the face of a deadly fire from the enemy's rifle-pits, when the Vermont regiments moved briskly up to his support, the Fourth regiment, under Major Pratt, taking and holding the front line. The Fourth regiment remaining in its position, General Grant returned to the center, where he was joined by the residue of the brigade, under Colonel Seaver, and the whole, except the Sixth Regiment, which was held in reserve, were put into the engagement.

"This was the important point for both armies, and the fighting here, upon both sides, was of the most desperate character. It was a hand-to-hand fight. The combatants were separated only by a breastwork of logs and rails, and they fired into each other's faces, and frequently clubbed their muskets to make or repel assault. In this way the brigade was engaged for about eight hours, when they were relieved and marched to the rear. The loss of the brigade was heavy, but the works were held."

On the 13th a portion of the brigade was engaged in skirmishing. On the 15th the Eleventh Vermont Regiment, with about fifteen hundred effective men, joined the brigade, and two companies of drafted men, who had been on duty at Brattleboro' for several months, were added to the Sixth Regiment.

On the 16th, Colonel Seaver, with his own and a Massachusetts regiment, made a reconnoissance in the direction of Spottsylvania Court House, driving the enemy's skirmishers into the main line of their works in a most gallant manner.

On the morning of the 18th, the Second and Sixth Corps charged the enemy's works, advancing about half a mile under heavy artillery fire. The Vermont Brigade had the front for some time, when the whole were ordered to retire. Colonel Warner, of the Eleventh, was severely wounded in this charge.

On the 19th, 20th, and 21st there was some heavy skirmishing, in which the Vermont Brigade participated, taking several prisoners. On the evening of the 21st, the Sixth Corps marched towards Guinea's Station.

The total loss of the Brigade, from the 4th of May, when they crossed the Rapidan, to the 21st, was sixteen hundred and fifty, as follows:—

Regiments.	Killed.	Wounded.	Missing.	Total.
Second,	80	340	34	454
Third,	48	243	33	324
Fourth,	46	229	33	308
Fifth,	38	229	51	318
Sixth,	35	176	19	230
Eleventh,	2	14	00	16
Totals,	249	1231	170	1650

When the original regiments of the Brigade crossed the Rapidan, on the 4th of May, it numbered twenty-eight hundred men, out of which they lost sixteen hundred and thirty-four — more than half its entire number in seventeen days.

On the 1st of June the Brigade participated in the battle of Cold Harbor, holding the extreme left of the line of the Sixth and Eighteenth Corps. Major Fleming's Battalion, and Captain Sears' Company, of the Eleventh Regiment, made a gallant charge upon the enemy's works, under a destructive fire. They were unsupported, and did not carry the works, but held the ground they had gained. On the 2d the Brigade changed its position, and was for a time under a heavy fire from the enemy.

"Early on the morning of the 3d a general but unsuccessful attack was made upon the enemy's works. In front of the Vermont Brigade were two regiments, in line of battle, under General Wheaton, and as these regiments advanced, the Brigade moved up promptly to their support. Colonel Seaver advanced his Third Regiment to the front line, and relieved one of General Wheaton's regiments, and soon after the Fifth Regiment was advanced, and relieved the other regiment in the front line. The Third and Fifth Regiments were greatly exposed, having no protection except the trees in the edge of the woods, and suffered very severely. They were subsequently withdrawn, and a skirmish line left in their place, which held the position the remainder of the day."

The casualties of the Brigade, from the 21st of May to the 4th of June, were two hundred and eighty, in which the Eleventh Regiment suffered most, its killed, wounded, and missing being one hundred and thirty-four. Captain Merrill T. Samson, of the Fifth Regiment, Lieutenant Hiram C. Bailey, of the Second, and Lieutenant Henry C. Miller, of the Third, all valued and brave officers, fell in the engagement of the 3d of June.

The Brigade held the front line from the 3d to the 11th of June. On the night of the 12th they started on the march for Petersburg. It had been under an incessant fire of musketry and artillery for twelve days. The front line was constantly engaged, the regiments occupying the front line by turns, a change being made every night. They engaged the enemy by day, and advanced by parallels, and strengthened their works by night.

The casualties in the Brigade, from the 4th to the 10th of June, were, in killed, wounded, and missing, forty-eight. Those in the Eleventh Regiment were nineteen. Major Richard B. Crandall, of the Sixth Regiment, a brave young officer, fell in front of the enemy's works on the 7th of June.

BATTLE OF PETERSBURG.

The Vermont Brigade crossed the Chickahominy on the 13th of June, 1864, the James River on the 16th, and arrived near Petersburg on the afternoon of the

17th, and that night occupied the rebel works, which had been carried that day. On the morning of the 18th there was a general attack upon the rebel lines, when it was found that they had fallen back to a new position during the night. In the afternoon our troops made an attack, and drove the enemy still further back. The Vermont Brigade, except the Second and Fifth Regiments, which held the skirmish line, were held in reserve, and did not participate in the engagement until night, when it was placed in the front line, and held it during the next day, skirmishing with the enemy, and under a heavy artillery fire. On the 20th the Brigade relieved General Gibbon's Division of the Second Corps, and held the position during the day, the front lines being engaged. The casualties from the 11th to the 20th of June were, in killed, wounded, and missing, thirteen.

On the 23d Captain Beattie, of the Third Regiment, with about ninety picked men, pushed forward to the Weldon Railroad, and a portion of the pioneers of the Brigade went on to the road and commenced its destruction. The Fourth, and Major Fleming's Battalion, of the Eleventh Regiment, occupied an advanced position as skirmishers. The enemy attacked the party upon the railroad, and drove them back, closed in from both sides upon the rear of the Fourth Regiment and Major Fleming's Battalion, making their escape impossible. Though the men fought with desperation to the last moment, and until their ammunition was exhausted, they were finally compelled to surrender.

In this encounter, Captain William C. Tracy, of the Fourth Regiment, was killed, and his body found upon the field the next day. Lieutenant Merritt H. Sherman, of the Eleventh Regiment, was killed during the day. He was a brave and worthy young officer. The Fourth Regiment lost in prisoners one hundred and thirty-nine officers and men, and the Eleventh, two hundred and sixty-three.

On the 29th of June the Vermont Brigade led the advance of the Sixth Corps to Ream's Station, on the Weldon Railroad, met the enemy, and drove them from the field. They marched to City Point on the 8th of July, and on the 9th embarked for Washington. On the 11th they participated in the engagement near Fort Stevens, with the rebels who made a demonstration upon Maryland and the City of Washington.

The Brigade remained in and near Washington until the 26th of July, when they marched to Harper's Ferry, and encamped on Bolivar Heights the night of the 29th. They were engaged in a slight skirmish on the 14th of August, near Strasburg, in which two men of the Second Regiment were wounded.

On the 21st of August the Brigade was engaged hotly with the enemy at Charlestown, Va., from nine o'clock in the morning until night. Lieutenant Colonel George E. Chamberlain, of the Eleventh Regiment, was wounded early in the day, while gallantly leading his men, and died soon after. He had recently been promoted, and was a young officer of great promise, much respected by his command and at home. Lieutenant Colonel Oscar A. Hale, and Major Carlos W. Dwinnell, of the Sixth Regiment, were severely wounded. Major Dwinnell, a valued young officer, died of his wounds on the 24th. The whole number of killed, wounded, and missing in the Brigade in this engagement was one hundred and twenty-three, the Sixth and Eleventh Regiments suffering most severely.

On the 13th of September the Brigade had a skirmish with the enemy at Opequan River, in which they lost one man killed, and seven wounded.

On the 19th, near Winchester, Va., the Vermont Brigade was again hotly engaged, under command of Colonel James N. Warner, of the Eleventh Regiment. In this engagement, as on all other occasions, the Brigade distinguished itself for coolness and bravery. It was in the thickest of the fight most of the day, which resulted in a signal victory to our arms. Colonel Warner, in his report of the engagement, says, " Were

I to report by name all the officers who distinguished themselves on this day, I should accompany this report by a roster of the commissioned officers of the Brigade. I cannot omit, however, the following commanding officers of regiments: Major E. E. Johnson, Second Vermont; Major Aldace Walker, Eleventh; Major H. W Floyd, commanding Third and Fourth; Captains A. Brown, Jr., Fifth, and M. W Davis, Sixth Regiments, all of whom did their duty nobly. Lieutenant Colonel A. S. Tracy, Second Vermont, who superintended a portion of the line, is entitled to great credit for being on the field on this occasion, as he was suffering from a severe disability. Captain A. H. Newt, A. A. A. G., Adjutant S. H. Lincoln, A. A. J. G., who was wounded early in the day, and Lieutenant H. C. Baxter, A. D. C., are deserving of special mention for their gallantry and coolness under fire. The accompanying list of casualties, which includes many of our best officers and men, is evidence of the stubbornness of the fighting in our front."

The casualties to the Brigade in this engagement, in killed, wounded, and missing, were two hundred and fifty-six. Captain Charles Buxton and Lieutenant Dennis Duhigg, of the Eleventh Regiment, were killed. Both these officers had recently been promoted, the former to major, and the latter to captain;

but their commissions, though forwarded, had not been received at the time of their death.

The term of service of the Second Regiment expired on the 19th of June, 1864, and on the 22d it was mustered out of service at Brattleboro', with two hundred and nineteen officers and men. The term of the Third expired July 15, 1864, and on the 27th of that month it was mustered out at Burlington, with one hundred and sixty officers and men. The term of the Fourth expired September 20, 1864, and on the 27th it was mustered out of service, at Brattleboro', with one hundred and forty-six officers and men. The organization of the Fifth Regiment was preserved by the re-enlistment of the requisite number of men. The term of service of the original members expired on the 15th of September, 1864, and such of the men as had not re-enlisted were mustered out of the service as a detachment, in the field, on that day, and returned to Burlington for final payment. The Second, Third, and Fourth, though mustered out as regiments, were each represented in the field by a large number of men who had joined the regiments at different times after its organization, and preserved their organization and numeric designations.

The following table shows the losses of the original regiments of the "Vermont Brigade," from September 30, 1863, to October 1, 1864:—

Regiments.	Mustered out of service.	Transf. to Veteran Res. Corps.	Disch'd.	Deserted.	Died.	Total.
Second,	219	35	50	39	133	476
Third,	160	29	44	66	127	426
Fourth,	146	25	33	50	123	377
Fifth,	00	22	21	30	89	162
Sixth,	00	51	38	35	94	218
Totals,	525	162	186	220	566	1659

BATTLE OF CEDAR CREEK.

On the 19th of October, 1864, just before daybreak, the enemy, in great force upon the easterly side of Cedar Creek, under Early, made a sudden and unexpected attack upon our forces, routing and driving them back in great confusion, and capturing a large number of guns and prisoners. The Union troops rallied, however, the Vermont Brigade advancing with the Sixth Corps, which became engaged in a desperate conflict, checking for a time the impetuous advance of the enemy. The troops on the right gave way, and the Division fell back a short distance to a crest, and formed a new line, the Vermont Brigade holding the center of its Division.

The enemy advanced in heavy force, drove in the skirmishers, and attacked the line of battle, but met with a severe repulse. The attack fell mainly upon the Vermont Brigade. General Ricketts, who commanded the Sixth Corps, was severely wounded, and General Getty, who commanded the Second Division, assumed the command of the Corps; General L. A. Grant took command of the Division; and Lieutenant Colonel Tracy, of the Second Regiment, took command of the Brigade.

The enemy made another attack, and were again severely repulsed, losing many men. A portion of the Union line finally gave way, and the enemy rushed through a piece of woods and opened a heavy fire upon our forces, driving back some of them, when the residue of the Division was ordered to retire. They retreated about half a mile, and took up a new position. The enemy followed, keeping up an incessant fire of artillery. The tide of battle seemed to be against the Union troops; the loss of men and guns had been very heavy, and a portion of our army had retreated in great confusion. The Sixth Corps had steadily and gallantly resisted the advance of the enemy, giving an opportunity to reform the line, which was done, with the Eighth Corps upon the left, the Sixth in the center, and the Nineteenth upon the right. The rebels made a vigorous attack, mostly upon the left and center of the Union line. The Sixth Corps held its ground; but the whole line was giving way, and the enemy pressed them back towards Newtown.

The Adjutant General's report, for 1865, says, "At this crisis, General Sheridan, who was at Winchester at the commencement of the battle, arrived upon the field. He rode rapidly down the pike and between the Third and Second Brigades, and, halting in front of the Second, inquired what troops they were. 'The Sixth Corps!' 'The Vermont Brigade!' was shouted almost simultaneously from the ranks. 'We are all right!' he exclaimed; and, swinging his hat over his head, he rode rapidly to the right, amid the exultant shouts of the men."

After a short cessation of firing, the Union troops were ordered to attack the enemy, and the Vermont Brigade moved forward under a heavy fire. The First and Third Brigades advanced at the same time — the First on the right, and the Third on the left, and both fell back under the severe fire of the enemy, while the Vermont Brigade took position behind a stone wall, refusing to retire, opened a heavy fire upon the rebels in front, and held the position far in advance of the other troops. "The enemy began to give way, and a movement upon the right being apparent, the Brigade sprang over the stone wall, advancing rapidly through an open ravine, and took position behind another stone wall, from which the enemy had been driven. The enemy made another stand, and the Brigade poured into their ranks a terrible fire of musketry. The Third Brigade, having reformed, took position upon the left of the Vermont Brigade. The enemy gave way, another advance was ordered, and there was no halt until the enemy had been driven across Cedar Creek, and the cavalry had taken up the pursuit: it was the last victorious charge of the day. The distance from the point of attack to Cedar Creek was about three miles, most of the way through an open country. The enemy's lines were entirely broken, and went back in great confusion. They were rapidly followed, and men rushed forward upon the double-quick, those who could move the most rapidly being found at the front. As the Brigade approached Cedar Creek, they were passed by two regiments of cavalry, one of which was the First Vermont, and the infantry then halted and reorganized. In this organization the Vermont Brigade was found in advance of all other troops, except the cavalry, which had just passed. The engagement and pursuit had continued from early morning until dark; and the Vermont Brigade, fatigued, but victorious, marched back, and encamped upon the same ground they had left in the moruing."

The following were the casualties in the Brigade during this engagement: —

Regiments.	Killed.	Wounded.	Missing.	Total.
Second,	3	31	4	38
Third,	3	38	1	42
Fourth,	6	20	3	29
Fifth,	2	17	3	22
Sixth,	5	32	11	48
Eleventh,	9	74	29	112
Totals,	28	212	51	291

Later reports increased the number of killed to 33, and reduced the number of wounded to 210, and of missing to 41; total, 284.

Among the killed was Second Lieutenant Oscar R. Lee, of the Eleventh Regiment. He had just been commissioned captain, but had not been mustered on his commission. He was a brave young officer. General Grant, in his report of the engagement, says, " I desire to commend for their good conduct the regimental commanders, and the officers and men in their respective commands."

The Brigade marched to Kearnstown, where they remained doing picket duty until the 9th of December, when, with the Sixth Corps, they went to Washington by railroad, and by water, on the 10th, to City Point, thence by rail to Mead's Station, and on the 13th upon the Squirrel Level road, and occupied the works previously held by the Fifth Corps, and went into winter quarters. The near proximity of the two lines made the picket duty, during a portion of the winter, quite arduous, one tenth of the entire command being required to remain in the trenches during the night.

On the 25th of March, 1865, just before daybreak, the enemy made an attack upon Fort Steadman. The Brigade remained in the works, expecting an attack in their front, and prepared to give the rebels a warm reception, until one o'clock, P M., when they moved to the left and front of Fort Fisher, where the Brigade was formed as an assaulting column, the Sixth Regiment being upon the left of the front line. " The Brigade, with other troops, charged over an open field, upon the enemy's strongly-intrenched picket-line, capturing nearly his whole force. In this affair, both officers and men behaved with their usual gallantry." The casualties in the Brigade were, four killed, thirty-three wounded. The engagement continued until eight o'clock P M., when the Brigade returned to their quarters. The captured picket line was held by our troops.

On the 27th of March before daybreak, a small column of the enemy made another attack upon our picket line, which was repulsed after a sharp skirmish. The casualties to the Brigade were, wounded, twenty-three; missing, twenty-two. Second Lieutenant Charles H. Carleton, of the Fourth Regiment, was among the wounded.

On the 2d of April the Brigade was again fiercely engaged with the enemy, in what proved to be the final battle of the great war, resulting as it did in the evacuation of Petersburg and Richmond on that day, and the surrender, on the 9th, of Lee's entire army to General Grant.

Early in this engagement General L. A. Grant was severely wounded in the head, and the command of the Brigade devolved upon Lieutenant Colonel A. S. Tracy, of the Second Regiment.

The troops having been properly disposed for an attack upon the enemy's works, — the initiative having been assigned to the Vermont Brigade, — at four o'clock, at the appointed signal from Fort Fisher, it moved briskly over the works of the skirmish line, and pressed silently forward. When near the enemy's first line of intrenchments, being discovered, they were met by a confused fire from the rebels, who fled in great disorder. The command then, with their accustomed battle-cry, charged forward for the enemy's main works, about five hundred yards in their front. They had passed about half the distance, when the enemy opened a well-directed fire of musketry from the front, and artillery from forts on either hand, which caused the line to waver for a moment only, when it again pressed forward with unsurpassed gallantry. "Officers and men vied with each other in the race for the works, and all organization was lost in the eagerness and enthusiasm of the troops. The abatis were passed, and the men swarmed over the works with exultant shouts, the rebels fleeing in all directions. The earthworks, one to the right of the ravine, containing four guns, and the other to the left, containing two guns, were captured."

"The honor of being the first to break the enemy's line is claimed by the Vermont Brigade; and the commanding officers of the Fifth, Sixth, and Eleventh Regiments each claim that their colors were first planted on the works. And it is claimed that Captain Charles G. Gould, of the Fifth Regiment, was the first man of the Sixth Corps, to mount the works. His regiment was in the first line of the Brigade, and in the charge he was far in advance of his command. Upon mounting the works he received a severe bayonet wound in the face, and was struck several times with clubbed muskets, but bravely held his ground, killing with his saber the man who bayoneted him, and retiring from the works only after his comrades had come to his assistance and routed the enemy from their lines."

The enemy retreated in hot haste for the woods in the rear, and were pursued by our troops. At the edge of the woods the Brigade was again formed in line, the regiments in their numerical order from right to left. The whole command pushed forward vigorously through thickets, swamps, and dense woods, losing all organization in the eagerness of the men to surpass each other in the pursuit of the rebels, who were so closely followed that they could scarcely fire a shot. They had abandoned all idea of resistance, and seemed only desirous to be taken prisoners. The pursuit continued for about four miles to near Hatcher's Run.

"The conduct of the officers and men in this second charge is represented to have been above all praise; singly, or in squads of three or four, the men would charge upon whatever obstructions came in their way. Brevet Major Elijah Wales, of the Second Regiment, with two men, captured a piece of artillery, turned it upon the enemy, and fired upon them the charge which they had themselves placed in the gun. Major William J. Sperry, of the Sixth Regiment, and Lieutenant George A. Bailey, of the Eleventh Regiment, assisted by a few men, captured two pieces, and turned them upon the retreating rebels. Unable to procure primers, the pieces were discharged by firing a musket into the vent. In this manner twelve rounds were fired, when a section of artillery coming up, the guns were turned over to its commander. Captain George G. Tilden, of the Eleventh Regiment, with about a dozen men, captured two pieces of artillery, eleven commissioned officers, and sixty-two enlisted men, of the Forty-second Mississippi Regiment. Sergeant Lester G. Hock, Company F, Fifth Regiment, charged a squad of rebels who surrounded a stand of colors, knocked down the color-bearer, and captured the colors. Corporal Charles W Dolloff, Company K, Eleventh Regiment, also captured a stand of colors."

There are hundreds of instances of gallantry and daring by officers and men of the famous Vermont Brigade, which never have been, and probably never will be, recorded in history. Their deeds of bravery during the four years of the Great Rebellion, would, if written out, make a volume of inconvenient size. Enough is known and recorded, however, to reflect upon it as high a degree of honor for faithfulness, endurance, and gallantry as has been accorded to any similar organization in the great and unsurpassed army engaged in putting down the most gigantic rebellion of the world.

The Brigade went into camp for the night in intrenchments which they threw up in Petersburg. The headquarters of the Brigade were established at the Turnbrell House, where General Robert E. Lee, the great rebel general, had had his headquarters for the winter.

The captures of the Brigade, during the day, comprised two battle-flags, nineteen pieces of artillery, horses, harnesses and equipments, great quantities of quartermasters' and medical stores, and several hundred prisoners. The casualties in the Brigade during the day, were twenty-six killed, one hundred and sixty-one wounded, seven missing; making a total of one hundred and ninety-four. The Second, Fifth, and Eleventh Regiments suffered the most. Among the killed were Captain Charles C. Morey, of the Second Regiment, and Lieutenant George O. French, of the Eleventh Regiment, both excellent officers and worthy men.

The Brigade, with the Sixth Corps, started in pursuit of the retreating rebel army early on the morning of the 3d of April, and came up with them at Sailor's Creek, about five o'clock on the afternoon of the 6th, when an engagement took place, in which the Vermont troops did not participate. The enemy were routed. In the evening of the same day, Colonel Tracy, with the Second, and a regiment from the First Brigade, had an engagement with the enemy, which resulted in completely driving the enemy from the front, and leaving Colonel Tracy in possession of the ground. He reports that the last shot fired at the enemy by the Sixth Corps was fired by the Second Vermont Regiment in this engagement.

After the surrender of the rebel army, on the 9th of April, the Brigade marched to Danville, Va., a distance of one hundred and five miles, in a little more than four days. From there they moved to Manchester, Va., and thence to Munson's Hill, Va., near

Washington, D. C., where they remained until mustered out of service.

SEVENTH REGIMENT.

The Seventh Regiment was successively commanded by Colonels George T. Roberts, of Rutland, who died August 7, 1862, of wounds received in action at Baton Rouge, two days before; William C. Holbrook, of Brattleboro', resigned June 2, 1865; David B. Peck, mustered out of service as lieutenant colonel, August 26, 1865; Henry M. Porter, of Middlebury, mustered out as lieutenant colonel with the regiment, March 14, 1866. The two latter were commissioned as colonels, but for want of a sufficient number of men were not mustered as such.

This regiment was engaged in the following battles: —

Siege of Vicksburg,	June and July, 1862.
Baton Rouge,	August 5, 1862.
Gonzale Station,	July 15, 1864.
Spanish Fort,	March 27 to April 11, 1865.
Whistler,	April 13, 1865.

This Regiment was mustered into the United States service at Brattleboro', on the 12th of February, 1862, and was sent to Ship Island, and subsequently moved to New Orleans. The men suffered severely from exposure during the unsuccessful attack upon Vicksburg, and afterward in camp. Two hundred and eighty-five of the men died previous to December 1, 1862. They were moved to Pensacola, and a portion of the companies garrisoned Fort Pickens. A portion of the regiment was engaged in the battle of Baton Rouge, August 5, 1862, and fought bravely, during which its Colonel, George T. Roberts, was mortally wounded, and died two days afterward. An attempt was made to show that the regiment behaved badly on that occasion; but an investigation, demanded by its officers, into the facts, proved the contrary, and that Vermont need not blush for the conduct of her Seventh Regiment.

The regiment was stationed in the District of West Florida, in the Department of the Gulf, up to August, 1864, performing garrison and picket duty by detachments. It had very little service as a body. In January, 1864, Lieutenant Ross, with Company B, was ordered to Point Washington, at the head of Choctawhotchie Bay, to protect and forward refugees wishing to enter our lines and enlist in our army. He advanced twenty-five miles into the interior, and captured a company of rebel infantry, of about fifty, that had been stationed there to prevent refugees and deserters escaping to our lines. While returning to Point Washington, he was surprised by a superior force of rebel cavalry, and captured, with eleven of his men and all his prisoners.

In February, 1864, all the original men in this regiment, except fifty-eight, re-enlisted. The re-enlisted men were given a furlough, and the others were mustered out at the end of the term of their enlistment. On the departure of the regiment for home, August 10, 1864, the re-enlisted men for furlough and the others to be mustered out, General Asboth, commanding officer of the West District of Florida, issued a complimentary order, in which he said, "The Seventh Vermont Veteran Volunteers, being about to leave this district, the general commanding considers it his pleasant duty to express his full appreciation of the good order and discipline always maintained, and efficient service constantly rendered by them, not only as infantry, at their several posts and in the field, but also most conspicuously as artillerists, at the important forts of Pickens and Barrancas."

On the 27th of September, the furloughs of the re-enlisted men having expired, they assembled at Brattleboro', and on the 30th departed for New Orleans, where they remained until February, 1865, when they embarked for Mobile Point, Alabama, where they remained until the 17th of March, and then left for Spanish Fort, before which it arrived on the 27th, and was attached to the Third Division, Thirteenth Army

Corps, and was several times engaged in heavy skirmishing, and under severe fire of artillery and musketry.

During the last few days of the siege of Spanish Fort, the regiment assisted in putting the siege guns in position, and making approaches. The officers and men, in every instance, behaved with great gallantry. The casualties in the regiment from March 19 to April 11 were eighteen wounded, and twenty-five captured.

On the 12th of April the regiment, with its division, marched through Mobile, and thence to Whistler, a station on the Mobile and Ohio Railroad, about six miles from Mobile, where they found a body of rebel cavalry, who retreated after a brisk skirmish.

The regiment went to Clarksville, Texas, and remained there, and in other places in that State, doing guard and other duty, until the 14th of March, 1866, when it was mustered out of service with twenty-two commissioned officers and three hundred and twenty-six enlisted men, and returned to Brattleboro', where they arrived on the 5th of April, and were paid and discharged.

EIGHTH REGIMENT.

This regiment was mustered into service on the 18th of February, 1862, and was successively commanded by Colonels Stephen Thomas, of West Fairlee, who was promoted to brigadier general February 1, 1865, and John B. Mead, of Randolph, who was mustered out with the regiment.

This regiment was engaged in the following battles:—

Cotten,	January 14, 1863.
Bisland,	April 2, 1863.
Siege of Port Hudson,	May 25 to July 9, 1863.
Winchester,	September 19, 1864.
Fisher's Hill,	September 21 and 22, 1864.
Cedar Creek,	October 19, 1864.
Newtown,	November 11, 1864.

The Eighth Regiment left the State on the 6th of March, 1862, with one thousand and fifteen officers and men; joined General Butler's expedition, and went to New Orleans, and were stationed at Algiers, opposite that city, during the summer of 1862, detachments being stationed temporarily at different points, and sent out on expeditions as occasion required.

On the 4th of September, 1862, a detachment from this regiment was engaged in a heavy skirmish with the enemy at Bayou des Allemands, where the loss amounted to sixteen killed, twenty wounded, and one hundred and thirty-seven missing. Among the missing were Captain Edward Hall and Lieutenant Andrew J. Sargent, of Company E, and Lieutenants Greene and Mead, of Company G. Of those who fell into the hands of the enemy, seven were shot by the rebels on the 23d of October as deserters, four died at Vicksburg, two were held as hostages, two were held as deserters, and one hundred and twenty-two, with their officers, were paroled.

During the siege of Port Hudson the regiment distinguished itself for coolness and bravery whenever brought into action. They participated in the assault on the 27th of May, and also on the 14th of June, 1863, showing the same gallantry that distinguished Vermont troops everywhere during the war. The casualties in the regiment during the siege were twenty-four killed, one hundred and twenty wounded, and two missing.

On the 1st of April that portion of the regiment which had re-enlisted was ordered home to receive their furlough, arriving in the State on the 15th. The residue remained at Algiers, under command of Major John L. Barstow, until the 6th of May, when they removed to Thibodeaux, a distance of sixty miles. On the 3d of June they were rejoined by those who had been home on furlough; and on the 5th, the original members of the regiment, who had not re-enlisted, were ordered to Vermont to be mustered out of service.

On the 5th of July the regiment left New Orleans, and arrived at Washington, D. C., on the 13th, and marched to Tenallytown, thence to Snicker's Gap, and back to Chain Bridge on the 23d. It was attached to the Nineteenth Corps, constituting a part of the army under Sheridan.

On the 19th of September the Eighth Regiment was engaged in the battle of Opequan Creek, near Winchester, fighting bravely and nobly, every officer and man doing his whole duty. Co. F were sent forward as skirmishers; Co. D, Captain Getchell, and Co. K, Captain Ford, were sent to the right, to occupy a space beyond the right of the Brigade. The remainder of the regiment were sent to the front, with the Twelfth Connecticut, and took position in an open field, the enemy occupying the woods in front, from which they had a short time before driven the Second Division, within rifle range. "Their fire of musketry and artillery was very heavy. The position was held for more than three hours, and until the Eighth Corps, under Major General Crook, were seen nearly a mile to the right, charging upon the enemy. Then Colonel Thomas, without waiting for orders, moved forward with the Eighth, and Twelfth Connecticut, at double-quick, charging and driving the enemy from the woods. After passing through the woods, the regiment halted, and was rejoined by Companies D, F, and K. The enemy were in force about four hundred yards to the left, behind a rail-fence, and the regiment wheeled to the left, firing deadly volleys upon them, and they soon took to flight. The residue of the Brigade came up, and the Eighth Regiment, with the One Hundred and Sixtieth New York, charged and drove the enemy from behind a stone wall. The pursuit continued until dark, when the regiment bivouacked, receiving the congratulations of Major General McMillan and Colonel Thomas for their gallant conduct. The loss during the day was eight killed and thirty wounded. Among the wounded was Lieutenant Colonel Henry F. Dutton, who was wounded early in the action."

The Eighth was with its brigade, engaged in the pursuit of the enemy, from the 20th to the 25th, and encamped at Harrisburg, having been engaged in charges and skirmishes nearly every day from the 19th to the 26th of September.

On the 6th of October the regiment moved from Harrisburg, and arrived at Cedar Creek on the 10th, where they encamped and fortified, and on the 19th was again hotly engaged with the enemy in the battle of Cedar Creek. During this engagement Colonel Thomas was in command of the brigade, and the command of the regiment devolved upon Major John B. Mead, who was wounded in the early part of the battle, and was succeeded by Captain McFarland. The loss during the day was one officer, Lieutenant Cooper, killed, and twelve officers wounded; Captain Hall, of Co. E, and Lieutenant Cheney, of Co. K, mortally; and fourteen enlisted men killed, and ninety-five wounded or taken prisoners.

The regiment returned to Cedar Creek, and on the 10th of November marched to Newtown, Va.; thence to Summit Point, where they remained through the winter, performing heavy guard and picket duty on the line of railroad from Charlestown to Winchester. On the 20th of February, 1865, a detachment of the regiment, while cutting timber, were attacked by guerrillas, and eleven men captured. They were soon paroled, and rejoined the regiment.

On the 21st of April the regiment proceeded by railroad to Washington, D. C., and encamped near Fort Stevens, where they remained through the month of May.

On the 1st of June the regiment was attached to the "Vermont Brigade," in the Sixth Corps, and participated in the review of the Vermont troops by the Governor of the State on the 7th, and also in the review of the Sixth Corps, by the President, on the 8th of June.

The regiment was mustered out of service on the 28th of June, and left Washington for Burlington, where they were discharged on the 10th of July.

Ninth Regiment.

The Ninth Regiment was mustered into the United States service on the 9th of July, 1862. It was successively commanded by Colonels George J. Stannard, of St. Albans, who was promoted to brigadier general, March 11, 1863; Dudley K. Andros, of Bradford, resigned May 22, 1863; and Edward H. Ripley, of Rutland, mustered out of service June 13, 1865. Colonel Ripley was breveted brigadier general, August 1, 1864.

The regiment was in the following engagements: —

Harper's Ferry,	September 13 and 16, 1862.
Newport Barracks,	February 2, 1864.
Chapin's Farm,	September 29, 1864.
Fair Oaks,	October 27, 1864.

The Ninth Regiment left the State on the 15th of July, 1862, with nine hundred and twenty officers and men. It proceeded to Washington, and thence to Winchester, Va., and was engaged in constructing fortifications. The regiment was captured at Harper's Ferry, on the 15th of September, 1862, when that post was surrendered, was paroled, and sent to Chicago, where it remained in parole camp until January 10, 1863, when the men were exchanged. They guarded rebel prisoners at that place until the following April, when it was removed to Fortress Monroe, thence to Suffolk, Va., West Point, Va., and Yorktown, Va., remaining there until the 24th of October, 1863, when they sailed for Newbern, N. C.

The regiment had become very much reduced in numbers by desertions, the men being dispirited for want of active duty, enlistments in the regular army, and malarial diseases.

They arrived at Newbern on the 29th of October, and were ordered to Newport Barracks, where they performed garrison duty, Colonel Edward H. Ripley, of the Ninth Regiment, commanding the post.

On the 2d of December the regiment met with a severe loss in the death of Charles Jarvis, of Weathersfield, who had been promoted to major. He died of wounds received in a skirmish, while endeavoring to capture a rebel party. On the 24th, Colonel Ripley, with a portion of his men and the One Hundred and Fifty-eighth New York regiment, went down the coast, destroyed extensive salt works, and brought in a number of negroes.

On the 31st of January, 1864, the regiment, with other troops, under the command of Colonel Jourdan, of the One Hundred and Fifty-eighth New York regiment, went on an expedition to Onslow County, N. C., and returned after an arduous march of seventy-five miles, having captured one rebel lieutenant and twenty-seven privates, with much valuable property.

On the 2d of February the enemy, with twenty-five hundred infantry, eight to twelve pieces of artillery, and four hundred cavalry, made an attack upon the outposts held by Companies H and B, Ninth Regiment. At that time the recruits, who had recently joined the regiment, were without arms, and the regiment numbered less than two hundred muskets. The recruits were soon armed, and hastily instructed how to load, and with pockets filled with cartridges, taken out upon the skirmish line, which was the only line that, from the open nature of the country and the great superiority of the enemy, could be opposed to them. A gallant resistance was made, and the position held until nearly dark, when the regiment fell back over the bridges, and burned them to prevent capture. In this movement the regiment lost two lieutenants and sixty-four men killed, wounded, and missing. Most of the missing were new recruits. The regiment was commanded by Captain Kelley, of Company B, Lieutenant Colonel Barney being in command of the post, and Colonel Ripley having just left for Fortress Monroe with prisoners and dispatches to General Butler.

On the 16th of March, Major Amasa Bartlett, of Irasburg, who had just received his commission, died. His loss was severely felt in the regiment. On the 26th of April, Captain Kelley, with twenty men, captured a fishing party of six men, sent out by the rebel commissary department, and destroyed valuable property. On the 29th, with forty men, he dashed into Swansboro', capturing a rebel lieutenant and sixteen men, with horses, arms, and a large quantity of government stores.

On the 11th of July the regiment moved to Newbern, and was assigned to duty at the various outposts. On the 31st of August the regiment was ordered to Bermuda Hundred, arriving there on the 15th of September, and was attached to the First Brigade, Second Division, of the Eighteenth Army Corps. They were joined on the 17th by one hundred and seventy recruits, making the effective strength of the regiment about eight hundred and seventy-five.

On the 29th of September the regiment left their camp, crossed the James River, and marched to Chapin's Farm. The Eighth Maine, and Ninth Vermont Regiments were ordered to charge one of the enemy's works. The Maine regiment became entangled in a swamp, and the Ninth Vermont charged alone, over uneven ground, covered with fallen timber and underbrush, carried the works, capturing two guns and over fifty prisoners, and driving the enemy from a line of rifle-pits connecting the captured fort with the works. The regiment was under fire the entire day, and every man behaved with great gallantry. The casualties in the regiment on this occasion were seven killed, thirty-eight wounded, and thirteen missing.

Early in November the regiment was sent to New York City, to assist in preserving order during the Presidential election, and were highly complimented for their good discipline amid the temptations of the city. They rejoined their Brigade on the 17th. In December the regiment was attached to the Second Brigade, Third Division, of the Twenty-fourth Corps.

A general order was issued from Corps Headquarters, dated January 17, 1865, providing for an inspection, at stated times, of the regiments in each brigade, with a view of determining which was the best regiment in the brigade; and then an inspection of the regiments, thus ascertained to be the best in each brigade, by the General commanding the Division, for the purpose of determining which was the best regiment in the Division. The Ninth Regiment entered into this competition with great spirit and determination, and by the perfection of their drill and discipline gained the post of honor in the Division, and the fact was announced at Division Headquarters. The Divison consisted of twenty regiments. The officers and men were justly proud of the distinction thus attained. When each of these complimentary orders were issued, the regiment was excused from all picket and outside details for one week. Before the period had terminated during which they had been excused from details, the men of the regiment made application to be allowed to go again upon duty, to relieve their comrades of the brigade, whose duties were rendered extremely arduous by the excusing of this regiment from details. This noble conduct called forth another complimentary order from Division Headquarters.

The Ninth Regiment was among the first to enter Richmond after its evacuation by the rebels, and was stationed there until mustered out. The original members of the regiment, and the recruits whose terms of service were to expire previous to the 1st of October, were mustered out on the 13th of June. The remaining members of the regiment were consolidated into a battalion of four companies, which remained in Virginia, performing ordinary camp, guard, and provost duty, until the 1st day of December, 1865, when they were mustered out of service, with twelve commissioned officers and three hundred and two enlisted men.

TENTH REGIMENT.

The Tenth Regiment was mustered into the United States service on the 1st day of September, 1862, and left the State on the 6th, with ten hundred and sixteen officers and men. It was successively command by Colonels Albert B. Jewett, of Swanton, who resigned April 25, 1864; William W. Henry, of Waterbury, who was wounded in May, 1864, resigned December 17, 1864, brevet brigadier general, March 7, 1865;

George B. Damon, of Newbury, who was mustered out of service after his regiment, as lieutenant colonel, June 28, 1865.

This regiment participated in the following engagements, in all of which the officers and men behaved with great gallantry, and fully sustained the credit of Vermont: —

Orange Grove,	November 27, 1863.
Wilderness,	May 5 to 10, 1864.
Spottsylvania,	May 10 to 18, 1864.
Tolopotomy,	May 31, 1864.
Cold Harbor,	June 1 to 12, 1864.
Weldon Railroad,	June 22 and 23, 1864.
Monocacy,	July 9, 1864.
Winchester,	September 19, 1864.
Fisher's Hill,	September 21 and 22, 1864.
Cedar Creek,	October 19, 1864.
Petersburg,	March 25, 1865.
Petersburg,	April 2, 1865.
Sailor's Creek,	April 6, 1865.

This regiment was brigaded with the Thirty-ninth Massachusetts, the Fourteenth New Hampshire, and the Twenty-third Maine regiments, and was, during the first year of its service, stationed on the Upper Potomac, near Poolsville, performing picket duty. During the invasion of Maryland and Pennsylvania by the rebels, the Tenth Regiment was attached to the Army of the Potomac, and formed a part of the Third Army Corps. When that corps was broken up it was attached to the First Brigade, Third Division, of the Sixth Army Corps, and with it participated in the engagement at Orange Grove, on the advance to Mine Run. They charged and drove the enemy in great confusion from a crest which they occupied, and which was held by the Tenth Regiment until after sunset, under a heavy fire from artillery and infantry at short range. The officers and men were highly commended for their good conduct on this occasion. The regiment lost nine killed, fifty-eight wounded, and Captain Dillingham, of Company B, was taken prisoner.

On the 4th of May, 1864, the regiment crossed the Rapidan with the Sixth Corps, and were under fire nearly every day until the 18th. Its loss during this time was four killed and twenty-three wounded.

On the 1st and 3d of June the regiment was actively engaged near Cold Harbor, and suffered severely. Lieutenant Colonel Henry, who was in command, was wounded on the 1st, and was succeeded by Major Charles G. Chandler. Lieutenants Ezra Stetson and Charles G. Newton, both valuable officers, were killed in the same action. On the 3d, Captain Edwin B. Frost was killed. His was a severe loss to the regiment. On the 6th, Captain Samuel Darrah, an intelligent and highly valued officer, was killed in front of regimental headquarters by a rebel sharpshooter. In all these engagements the officers and men of the Tenth Regiment behaved with great coolness and courage. The casualties were twenty-seven killed, one hundred and forty-seven wounded, and six missing.

On the 9th of July this regiment was in the battle of Monocacy Junction, and lost four men killed, twenty-six wounded, and thirty-two missing. They subsequently were joined to General Sheridan's army in the Valley of the Shenandoah, and were in the battle of Opequan Creek, near Winchester, on the 19th of September, behaving well, and losing thirteen killed and sixty wounded. Major Edwin Dillingham, a young, patriotic, and brave officer, was among the killed.

On the 19th of October the Tenth Regiment was engaged in the battle of Cedar Creek. The rebels had captured three of our pieces of artillery, and a charge was ordered by this regiment; and, with the colors in front, they advanced with alacrity, charged up to the guns, and recovered them. Sergeant William Mahoney, of Company E, color-bearer of the regiment, was the first to reach the guns, and planted the colors upon one of them. The rebels retired in great confusion. In this engagement the casualties in the regiment were fourteen killed, sixty-six wounded, and five missing, being nearly one third of the entire regiment. Among the killed were Captain Lucian D. Thompson and Color-Sergeant Mahoney.

On the 25th of March, 1865, this regiment was engaged near Fort Fisher, charged upon and captured the works of the enemy. They took one hundred and sixty prisoners, including several commissioned officers. In this action the regiment lost two men killed and four wounded.

On the 2d of April the Brigade, of which the Tenth Regiment formed a part, made another charge upon the works of the enemy, and succeeded in capturing them, with many prisoners and several guns. The commanding officer of the brigade, in his official report, said, "the first colors inside the works were those of the Tenth Vermont." The casualties in the regiment during the day were three killed, forty-one wounded, and four captured. Adjutant James M. Read was mortally wounded, and died four days after. He was a very promising young officer.

From Petersburg the regiment marched with the Sixth Corps to Sailor's Creek, where it was again engaged with the enemy on the 6th of April, taking part in the decisive flank movement which closed the action. The regiment then marched to Appomattox Court House, where the rebel army surrendered on the 9th of April. On the 23d they started for Danville, Va., and marched thence, a distance of over one hundred miles, in four days and four hours. They remained at Danville about three weeks, and then moved by way of Richmond to Washington, D. C., where they arrived about the 1st of June, went into camp near Ball's Cross Roads, and remained there until mustered out of service, June 22, 1865.

Eleventh Regiment.

The Eleventh Regiment was mustered into the United States service on the 1st day of September, 1862, and left the State on the 7th, with ten hundred and eighteen officers and men. The regiment was successively commanded by James M. Warner, who was made Brevet Brigadier General for gallantry at Spottsylvania Court House, Winchester, Fisher's Hill, and Cedar Creek, Va., to date from August 1, 1864; promoted to Brigadier General, May 8, 1865; and Charles Hunsden, of Stoneham, who was mustered out June 24, 1865.

By an order from the War Department, this regiment was changed from infantry to heavy artillery, and was stationed at Washington, D. C., occupying Forts Slocum, Totten, and Stevens. On the 15th of May they joined the "Vermont Brigade," after which its history is given with that organization.

Second Vermont Brigade.

This Brigade was composed of the Twelfth, Thirteenth, Fourteenth, Fifteenth, and Sixteenth Regiments — all enlisted for nine months.

The Twelfth Regiment was commanded by Asa P. Blunt, of St. Johnsbury; the Thirteenth by Francis V Randall, of Montpelier; the Fourteenth by William T. Nichols, of Rutland; the Fifteenth by Redfield Proctor, of Cavendish; the Sixteenth by Wheelock G. Veazey, of Springfield.

These regiments were brigaded together during their entire term of service. The Brigade was successively commanded by Brigadier General Edwin H. Stoughton, who was surprised and captured by the enemy; Colonel Asa P Blunt, of the Twelfth Regiment, until April, 1863, when Brigadier General George J. Stannard was assigned to its command, and so continued to the end of its term of service. The Brigade was stationed near Washington, performing picket duty, until June 25, 1863, when it was ordered to report to General Reynolds, commanding the First Army Corps, and joined the Corps at Gettysburg on the evening of July 1st, after a march of one hundred and twenty-five miles, in seven days, during much of the time through a heavy rain.

BATTLE OF GETTYSBURG.

In the early part of the summer of 1863, the rebel leaders proclaimed their intention of invading the North, and thus retaliate for the devastation occasioned by the war in Virginia and other States claimed by them as belonging to the Confederacy. They made no attempt at secrecy. Their plan, as understood, was to overwhelm Hooker's army, capture Washington, and make a grand raid into Pennsylvania, or some other fruitful and inviting section of the North, and carry away such horses, cattle, and supplies of all kinds as they needed, and destroy all else of value that fell in their way. General Hooker was aware of the programme agreed upon by the enemy, and was on the alert to meet him. Under his orders, General Pleasanton, with a cavalry force, made an attack upon General Stewart at Beverly Ford, captured his private papers, and compelled him to fall back and abandon his intention of harassing and diverting Hooker's advance. Among the captured papers was found a General Order for an advance into Pennsylvania.

To meet the threatened advance, General Hooker put his army in rapid motion. His troops were so disposed as to protect Washington, and also to give the enemy battle should he invade the Northern States at any point. No one knew precisely where the rebels would strike. Pennsylvania, Maryland, New Jersey, and New York were appealed to, and urged to rally for the protection of their respective borders, and they promptly and nobly answered the call. The last week of June was one of great anxiety and doubt. It was known that the rebel army, ninety-thousand strong, was making an advance upon the North, and must be met by an equal or superior force. It soon became apparent that the enemy was concentrating a very large force near Gettysburg, Pa., and on Monday night, the 29th of June, the troops under the rebel Generals Hill, Longstreet, and Ewell were encamped on the eastern slope of the mountain, in full view of that place.

On the 28th of June, General Meade assumed command of the Union army. He concentrated, as rapidly as possible, the troops under Generals Buford, Reynolds, and Howard, and they took positions on the south side, and near to the town, on the night of the 29th. A desperate battle was imminent. On the morning of Wednesday, July 1, General Buford was ordered to advance with his cavalry and occupy the town. He was met by the enemy, who immediately opened fire upon him; hearing which, General Reynolds, with the First Corps, of eight thousand men, weary with marching, dashed into and through the town, and commenced a vigorous attack upon twenty thousand fresh troops, which was met with equal vigor by the enemy. General Reynolds took a position, and not only stubbornly held it, but drove back the foe whenever they made a charge upon his lines. The rebels were re-enforced from time to time, until they numbered full forty thousand, while our own forces on the field were less than half that number. The brave General Reynolds was killed in the early part of the day. The contest raged furiously until near night, when it became evident that our troops could not much longer withstand the terrible fire of a foe so greatly superior in numbers, and a retreat was ordered.

Our men were driven back through the town by the howling and excited rebels, who took twenty-two hundred prisoners. Suddenly the artillery opened from a hill at the south, and checked and drove back the enemy.

The battle throughout the day, in every part of the field, had been among the fiercest and most terrible of the war. The fire on both sides was more terrific than veterans had ever seen before. One brigade of western troops, which, in the morning, numbered eighteen hundred and twenty, reached Cemetery Hill at night with but seven hundred men. Another brigade by its side went in with fifteen hundred men at noon, and came out at night having lost thirteen hundred and thirty-three privates, and fifty-four officers. This was carnage such as had not been witnessed upon any other field. The disparity in numbers was too great, and the Unionists were forced to yield the ground. Gettysburg was in the hands of the rebels, and all looked gloomy for the loyalists. The loss on both sides had been terrible, and the instances of bravery and daring by officers and men were almost without number.

Both armies passed the night in preparation for the morrow. Our men must be re-enforced, or they were lost. They went into the battle with less than half the number of the enemy, had suffered much more than he, and what remained were weary and disheartened. The rebels were exultant, and looked for an easy and decisive victory. Before midnight our men were cheered by the arrival of the Twelfth Corps, under General Slocum, and the Third, under General Sickles; and shortly after daylight on the 2d, came the Second and Fifth Corps. These accessions of strong men, and General Meade, with his confident bearing, to command the whole, inspired the men who had fought so nobly the day before, with new life and courage. All our troops were carefully and properly disposed, and ready for action. The rebels were not so exultant as the night before.

It was not until four o'clock in the afternoon of Thursday, July 2, that the enemy commenced the attack. Then followed such a battle as had not before been recorded in history. Volley succeeded volley, and charge followed charge. The gallantry displayed by men on both sides was unprecedented, and the slaughter terrible to contemplate or remember. The strife continued until night, without a decisive victory for either army. The rebels left the contest with their confidence considerably shaken, while our army felt strong in the rectitude of their cause. The night was spent by the men in needed rest, and by officers on both sides preparing for a renewal of the contest the next day.

At early dawn on Friday morning, the 3d of July, our guns opened fire upon the enemy. The battle continued from this time until eleven o'clock, when it entirely ceased until half past one. In the afternoon General Lee, who had been in command from the commencement of the battle, determined to make one more desperate attempt upon our left center, which was held by General Hancock. He made the attack with a heavy force, which was nobly met and splendidly repulsed. In speaking of it, Abbott, in his "History of the Civil War," says, "So fiercely they stormed the hill that the patriot General Gibbons was obliged to order his own men back to make room for the fatal grape. Volley after volley he poured into the surging mass; and, when the smoke cleared away, the brave charging lines were gone, not broken, not retreating, but gone — gone like leaves before the wind."

In this last day's battle our troops completely defeated and routed the enemy, captured six thousand and five hundred prisoners, their battery, and five thousand stand of arms. Before the next morning General Lee and his whole army had made good their retreat.

During the second day of the battle a battery fell into the hands of the rebels. The gunners had all been killed or fled. General Hancock had been unable to rally its supporters. He rode up to Colonel Randall, of the Thirteenth Vermont Regiment, whose horse had just been shot under him, and who was on foot at the head of his regiment, and asked him if he could retake that battery. "We can. Forward, boys!" was Colonel Randall's reply. He retook the battery, sent the guns to the rear, and advanced half a mile further to the front, and captured two twelve-pound brass guns.

The great feature of the battle of Gettysburg was the charge of Pickett's Division, so called. It was made, according to the best authority, with two whole divisions, and parts of others — in all about seventeen thousand men. It commenced in the afternoon of the third day, with a cannonade from about one hundred field-pieces, which were replied to by eighty guns from the Union forces. So heavy was the firing that it was heard distinctly at Greensboro', Pa., a distance, in a direct line, of one hundred and forty-three miles. The cannonading ceased, and then followed the grand charge.

The main body of the rebels were formed in two lines, with a front of about three hundred rods. The ground selected was an open meadow at the left of Cemetery Hill, on either side of which, on slightly elevated ground, were posted the opposing armies. The enemy advanced steadily, preceded by their skirmishers. The Vermont Brigade occupied an advanced position, and were ordered by General Stannard into line. The enemy's right seemed to be aiming directly upon the Fourteenth Regiment. Seeing which, General Stannard sent an order to Colonel Nichols to hold his fire until the rebels were close upon him, then to pour in a volley, and after that give them the bayonet. The rebel force suddenly charged, and marched across the front of the Brigade, about sixty rods, and again came upon the line of the Second Corps, at about eighty rods distance. The Fourteenth Regiment opened fire by battalion, and continued by files, and was soon joined by the Thirteenth, and, as a writer who was upon the ground says, "A line of dead rebels at the close showed distinctly where they marched across the front of the Vermont Second Brigade."

As the enemy pressed forward, General Stannard ordered the Thirteenth and Sixteenth Regiments to attack his flank. They moved up promptly to within half pistol range, and opened fire upon the column of the enemy, advancing after every volley. At this short range, the same writer says, "The Thirteenth fired ten or fifteen rounds, and the Sixteenth probably half that number, into a mass of men on which every bullet took effect, and many doubtless found two or three victims. The effect upon the rebel lines was instantaneous. Their progress ceased close upon the low breastworks of the Second Corps. For a moment they crowded together in bewilderment, falling like wheat before the reaper; then, breaking into a disorderly mob, they fled in all directions. The larger portion, on their right and center, dropped their arms, and rushed within our lines as prisoners."

The rebel brigade which formed the support of Pickett's division on his right, was now advancing across the open field directly upon the position of the Fourteenth Regiment. The batteries and the Fourteenth gave them a hot fire in front, while the Sixteenth was ordered to attack the flank. The rebel force was brought nearly to a halt by the fire in front. At this stage Colonel Veazey, of the Sixteenth, requested permission of General Stannard to make a charge, which was granted, and the Sixteenth, without firing a gun,

BATTLE OF GETTYSBURG.

rushed upon the enemy's flanks with bayonets. "The movement was so sudden that the rebel commander could effect no change of front to meet it, and the Sixteenth swept down the line of three regiments, taking their colors, and scooping them in a body into our lines."

The following is a portion of the report of Brigadier General Stannard, commanding the Second Vermont Brigade, dated "In front of Gettysburg, July 4, 1863": —

"We reached the battle-ground too late in the day to take part in the severely contested battle of July 1, and my tired troops upon their arrival took position in rear of the line of battle of the First Corps.

" Before reaching the ground, the Twelfth and Fifteenth Regiments were detached, by order of General Reynolds, as a guard to the Corps wagon train in the rear. The Fifteenth rejoined the Brigade next morning, but was again ordered back for the same duty, about noon of that day. After the opening of the battle on the 2d, the left wing of the Thirteenth Regiment, under Lieutenant Colonel Munson, was ordered forward, as support to a battery, and a company of the Sixteenth was sent out as support to the skirmishers in our front. While stationing them, Captain A. G. Foster, Assistant Inspector General of my staff, was seriously wounded by a ball through both legs, depriving me of his valuable services for the remainder of the battle. Just before dark of the same day, our army line on the left of the center having become broken, under a desperate charge of the enemy, my Brigade was ordered up. The right wing of the Thirteenth Regiment, under command of Colonel Randall, was in the advance, and upon reaching the breach in the line, was granted by General Hancock, commanding upon the spot, the privilege of making an effort to retake the guns of Company C, Regular Battery, which had just been captured by the enemy.

"This they performed in a gallant charge, in which Colonel Randall's horse was shot under him. Four guns of the battery were retaken, and two rebel field-pieces, with about eighty prisoners, were captured by five companies of the Thirteenth, in this single charge. The front line, thus reëstablished, was held by this Brigade for twenty-six hours. At about two o'clock of the 3d instant the enemy commenced a vigorous attack upon our position. After subjecting us, for an hour and a half, to the severest cannonade of the whole battle, from nearly one hundred guns, the enemy charged with a heavy column of infantry. The charge was aimed directly upon my command, but owing apparently to the firm front shown them, the enemy diverged midway, and came upon the line on my right. But they did not thus escape the warm reception prepared for them by the Vermonters. As soon as the change of the point of attack became evident, I ordered a flank attack upon the enemy's column. Forming in the open meadow in front of my line, the Thirteenth and Sixteeth Regiments marched down in column, by the flank, changed front forward, at right angles to the main line of battle of the army, bringing them in line of battle upon the flank of the charging column of the enemy, and opened a destructive fire at short range, which the enemy sustained but a very few minutes before the larger portion of them surrendered and marched in, not as conquerors, but as captives. They had hardly dropped their arms before another rebel column appeared, charging upon our left. Colonel Veazey, of the Sixteenth, was at once ordered back to take it, in its turn, upon the flank. This was done, as successfully as before. The rebel force already decimated by the fire of the Fourteenth Regiment, was scooped, almost en masse, into our lines. The Sixteenth took, in this charge, the regimental colors of the Second Florida and Eighth Virginia regiments, and the battle-flag of another rebel regiment.

"The Sixteenth was supported for a time, in the now advanced position it occupied after the charge, by four companies of the Fourteenth, under command of Lieutenant Colonel Rose.

"The movements I have described were executed in the open field, under a heavy fire of shell, grape, and musketry, and they were performed with the promptness and precision of battalion drill. They ended the contest on the center, and substantially closed the battle.

"Officers and men behaved like veterans, although it was, for most of them, their first battle, and I am content to leave it to the witnesses of the fight, whether or no they sustained the credit of the service, and the honor of our Green Mountain State.

"That their efforts were approved by the Division General, is shown by the General Order appended to this report.

"The members of my staff, Captain William H. Hill, Assistant Adjutant General; Lieutenant G. W Hooker, and Lieutenant G. G. Benedict, Aid-de-Camp; Lieutenant Clark, Provost Marshal, and Lieutenant S. F. Prentiss, Ordnance Officer, executed all orders with the utmost promptness, and their coolness under fire, and good example, contributed essentially to the success of the day."

On the 4th of July Major General Doubleday issued the following General Order:—

"The Major General commanding the Division desires to return his thanks to the Vermont Second Brigade, the One Hundred and Fifty-first regiment Pennsylvania Volunteers, and the Twentieth regiment New York State Militia, for their gallant conduct in resisting, in the front line, the main attack of the enemy upon this position, after sustaining a terrific fire from seventy-five to one hundred pieces of artillery. He congratulates them upon contributing so essentially to the glorious, and it is to be hoped, decisive victory of yesterday."

The losses in the Brigade during this battle were as follows: —

	Killed.	Wounded.	Missing.	Total.
Thirteenth Regiment,	8	89	26	123
Fourteenth Regiment,	17	68	22	107
Sixteenth Regiment,	14	89	15	118
Totals,	39	246	63	348

General Stannard was among the wounded in this engagement. One of his staff officers, in an article entitled "Vermont at Gettysburg," says, "During the last sharp shower of grape and shell with which the enemy strove to cover his repulse, General Stannard was wounded in the leg by an iron shrapnel ball, which passed down for three inches into the muscles on the inside of the thigh. His wound was very painful until a surgeon came — which was not for an hour — and removed the ball; but, though strongly urged, he refused to leave the field. He remained in front with his men till his command was relieved from duty in the front line, his wounded had been removed, and arrangements made for burying the dead, and then sank almost lifeless to the ground. To his perfect coolness, close and constant presence with his men, and to the promptness — almost that of inspiration — with which he seized the great opportunity of the battle, was very greatly owing the glorious success of the day."

The term of service of the Twelfth Regiment expired on the 4th of July, and it was mustered out of service on the 14th of July, 1863; the Thirteenth was mustered out on the 21st of July, 1863; the Fourteenth on the 30th of July, 1863; the Fifteenth on the 5th of August, 1863; and the Sixteenth on the 10th of August, 1863.

Seventeeth Regiment.

This Regiment was mustered into the United States service, by companies, in 1864, and was mustered out on the 14th of July, 1865. It was commanded by Colonel Francis V Randall, of Montpelier. It was engaged in the following battles: —

Wilderness,	May 6 to 9, 1864.
Spottsylvania,	May 12 to 15, 1864.
Spottsylvania,	May 18, 1864.
North Anna,	May 25 and 26, 1864.
Tolopotomy,	May 31, 1864.
Bethesda Church,	June 3, 1864.

Cold Harbor,	June 7 and 8, 1864.
Petersburg,	June 17, 1864.
Petersburg Mine,	July 30, 1864.
Weldon Railroad,	August 26, 1864.
Poplar Grove Church,	September 30, 1864.
Hatcher's Run,	October 27 and 28, 1864.
Petersburg,	April 2, 1865.

Companies A, B, C, D, E, F, and G, under command of Lieutenant Colonel Charles Cummings, of Brattleboro', left the State on the 18th of April, 1864. Company H joined the regiment on the 8th of June; Company I on the 13th of August, and was soon after followed by Company K. They joined the Second Brigade, Second Division, Ninth Army Corps, at Alexandria, Va., on the 22d of April. They were in the battle of the Wilderness from the 6th to the 9th of May On the 6th the regiment was under a heavy fire, during which Lieutenant Colonel Cummings was wounded in the head, and the command devolved upon Major William B. Reynolds. The officers and men behaved with remarkable coolness and gallantry in this and all the subsequent battles of the Wilderness, adding its share to the honor reflected upon Vermont by her troops in the field. The men were suffering from measles, and mustered but three hundred and thirteen muskets on the morning of the battle. The regiment lost nine men killed, sixty-four wounded, and seven missing.

At Spottsylvania, from the 12th to the 18th of May, the regiment fought with great bravery, losing ten men killed, and three officers and fifty-seven enlisted men wounded. On the 3d of June the regiment was again under heavy fire at Bethesda Church, during which Captain A. J. Davis, of Company B, a noble officer, was mortally wounded, and soon died. The casualties in the regiment from the 20th of May to the 6th of June, being under fire nearly every day, were two killed, and thirty-two wounded, three of whom died of their wounds. On the 16th of June they arrived near Petersburg, and on the 17th greatly distinguished themselves by a gallant charge upon the works of the enemy, which were carried. The regiment was highly complimented by General Burnside for the part it performed in the charge. It was in advanced works until the 20th, much of the time under fire. Casualties from the 8th to the 20th of June, ten killed and twenty-five wounded. Among the killed was Lieutenant Guy H. Guyer, a gallant officer. It was in constant active service from the 20th of June to the 29th of July, losing five men killed, and twenty-seven wounded.

The regiment, under Major Reynolds, was in the famous charge at Petersburg, on the 30th of July, after the blowing up of the enemy's forts by means of "mines," behaved gallantly, and lost every one of its commissioned officers — three killed, one wounded, four missing; enlisted men, three killed, twenty-three wounded, seventeen missing — aggregate loss, fifty-one. Among the killed were the gallant Major Reynolds, and Lieutenants William F Martin and John R. Converse, all brave officers.

On the 30th of September the regiment was in another severe engagement, opposite Petersburg, the officers and men sustaining their well-earned reputation for bravery. The casualties were, — officers, three wounded and missing; enlisted men, three killed, and forty-one wounded, and twenty-nine missing. Among the wounded and missing was Lieutenant Colonel Cummings. He fell into the hands of the enemy, and died of his wounds soon after.

In October, Company K joined the regiment, making the full complement of ten companies, and on the 27th Colonel Francis V Randall assumed the command. During the winter Colonel Randall was in command of Fort Davis, on the Jerusalem Plank Road, about two miles from Petersburg, and the Seventeenth was stationed there. On the morning of the 2d of April, 1865, it was hotly engaged in the assault upon Petersburg which resulted in its surrender. It was under the immediate command of Lieutenant Colonel Knapp, and all behaved with great bravery. The loss to the regiment was eight killed, thirty-nine wounded, and two missing. Among the killed was Lieutenant J. Edwin Henry, of Company K, a fine officer. Among the wounded was Lieutenant Colonel Lyman E. Knapp, Captain George S. Robinson, and Lieutenant Hollis O. Claflin.

The regiment joined in the pursuit of Lee's army, and, after its surrender, returned to Burkesville, where Colonel Randall was placed in command of the town. On being relieved here, the regiment moved to Alexandria, and was mustered out of service on the 14th of July, 1865.

Sharpshooters.

There were three companies of Sharpshooters raised in Vermont, and, with those sent from other States, proved a most valuable arm of the service. Their duties were most arduous, and often in positions of greatest danger. They were performed by individuals, detachments, and companies, where other troops could not be used either safely or effectively. They participated in more battles and skirmishes than the average of other troops, and probably sent more rebels into the presence of their Maker than the same number of men in other organizations. They were seldom used in line of battle in dense masses, and consequently suffered less loss in comparison than most other regiments.

SHARPSHOOTER.

Such was the nature of their duties, and the manner in which they performed them, that they received but a very small share of the glory of the war which was actually due them.

The First Company, F, was attached to the First Regiment United States Sharpshooters; the Second, E, and the Third, H, were attached to the Second Regiment United States Sharpshooters.

Company F was successively commanded by Edmund Weston, Jr., of Randolph, who resigned August, 2, 1862; Charles W. Seaton, of Charlotte, resigned May 15, 1863; Ezbon W Hindes, of Rutland, discharged for disability, November 7, 1863; and Charles D. Merriam, of Brattleboro', mustered out with the original members of the company, September 13, 1864.

Company E was successively commanded by Homer E. Stoughton, of Randolph, promoted to Major of his regiment, September 2, 1862; Francis D. Sweetzer, discharged for disability, September 14, 1863; and Seymour F. Norton, of Burlington, transferred with the veterans of his company to the Fourth Vermont Regiment, February 25, 1865.

Company H was successively commanded by Gilbert Hunt, of Dorset, resigned August 13, 1862; Albert Buxton, of Londonderry, killed in action at Wilderness, May 6, 1864; William Newell, of Dorset, honorably discharged, October 7, 1864, for wounds received in action before Petersburg, June 21, 1864; William H. Churchill, of Londonderry, killed in action before Petersburg, October 27, 1864; and Walter W. Smith, of Wilmington, transferred to Fourth Vermont Regiment, February 25, 1865.

Company F was in thirty-seven engagements, from Great Bethel, March 28, 1862, to Petersburg, October 27, 1864.

Companies E and H were in twenty-four engagements, from that at Orange Court House, August 4, 1862, to that at Hatcher's Run, December 5, 1864.

William Y. H. Ripley, of Rutland, was commissioned Lieutenant Colonel of the First Regiment Sharpshooters, January 1, 1862, and discharged for promotion, August 6, 1862. Homer R. Stoughton, of Randolph, was successively promoted from Captain of Company E, to Major, Lieutenant Colonel, and Colonel of the Second Regiment. He was wounded May 5, 1864, mustered out after the regiment was disbanded.

Company F was at Kelley's Ford, November 7, 1863, and with its regiment, numbering less than two hundred, forded the river, under a severe fire, in pursuit of the retreating enemy, and captured five hundred and six prisoners, of whom more than two hundred surrendered to Company F. At the Wilderness, on the 5th of May, 1864, it went into the fight with two officers and forty-three enlisted men. They were deployed as skirmishers on the left of the "Vermont Brigade." The men fought bravely, but were forced back, losing in five minutes' fighting thirteen of its number — five killed or mortally wounded, and two taken prisoners. The company was almost constantly engaged in fighting and skirmishing through the summer, every officer and man doing his duty well. On the 19th of September, their term of service having expired, those officers and men, twenty in all, who had not re-enlisted, were mustered out of service.

Companies F and H, attached to the Second Regiment, distinguished themselves on many occasions, through the summer and fall of 1863. They were engaged in the battles of the Wilderness, from the 5th to the 8th of May, 1864, both inclusive. Captain Buxton, of Company H, a most brave and worthy officer, was killed on the 6th. That company, also, lost four men killed, nineteen wounded, and two missing. From the 5th to the 18th of May the companies were almost constantly fighting and skirmishing. Company E lost three killed and twenty wounded; Company H, five killed, nineteen wounded, and two missing. On the 31st of May the regiment charged and carried the enemy's works, capturing nearly as many prisoners as there were men in the regiment. They were actively engaged at Petersburg, and Colonel Stoughton, who was in command of the regiment, was captured. They served in the Army of the Potomac until February, 1865, when they were transferred to the Fourth Vermont, and became Companies G and H of that regiment.

First Battery Light Artillery.

This Battery was mustered into the United States service February 18, 1862. It was commanded by George H. Duncan, of Shaftsbury, who resigned February 11, 1863; and George T. Hebard, of Chelsea, who was mustered out of service August 10, 1864, when the original members were mustered out, and the recruits transferred to the Second Vermont Battery.

The First Battery was in the following engagements: —

Siege of Port Hudson,	May 25 to July 9, 1863.
Pleasant Hill,	April 9, 1864.
Cane River,	April 23, 1864.
Bayou de Glaze,	May 18, 1864.

This Battery was stationed at Baton Rouge until the 21st of May, 1863, when it was moved to Port Hudson, and was engaged in the siege of that place, the men distinguishing themselves for their discipline, drill, and fighting qualities. During the following winter, several detachments were sent out from this Battery on reconnoisances and for other duty. At Pleasant Hill, on the 9th of April, 1864, they were charged upon by the enemy in force, and a severe fire of cannister was opened upon them at short range, which was gallantly repulsed. Captain Hebard, in his report, says that "even when the enemy were within fifty yards, and within speaking distance, not an officer or man left his post." The casualties were one man wounded, and five horses killed and wounded.

The Adjutant General, in his report for 1864, says, "The Battery has been greatly distinguished for its thorough discipline and the effectiveness of its drill, and the officers and men have had large experience in the dangers and vicissitudes of battle, and have on all occasions distinguished themselves for their cool daring and determined courage." Their term of service having expired, the Battery was mustered out of service, at Brattleboro', on the 10th of August, 1864.

SECOND BATTERY OF LIGHT ARTILLERY.

This Battery was mustered into the United States service December 24, 1861. It was commanded by Lensie R. Sales, of Leicester, who resigned February 20, 1862; Pythagoras E. Holcomb, of the Seventeenth

United States Infantry, who was promoted to Major of Texas Cavalry, August 19, 1863; and John W Chase, of Brandon, who was mustered out with the Battery. It was engaged in the following actions: —

Plain's Store, May 21, 1863.
Siege of Port Hudson, May 25 to July 9, 1863.

This Battery was stationed at Ship Island and New Orleans, served in the Department of the Gulf, and was in the siege of Port Hudson, the men fighting with coolness and courage. On the 31st of August, 1863, it was stationed at Port Hudson, performing garrison duty, and going by detachments on expeditions into the interior as occasion required, until September 20, 1864, when twenty of the men who did not re-enlist, whose term had expired, were mustered out of service. The Battery was largely re-enforced by recruits and transfers from the First Battery. It remained at Port Hudson until July, 1865, when it was mustered out of service.

THIRD BATTERY OF LIGHT ARTILLERY.

This Battery was mustered into the United States service January 1, 1864. It was commanded by Romeo H. Start, of St. Albans, during its whole term of service. It was in four engagements at Petersburg;

July 30, 1864; August 18, 1864; March 25, 1865; and April 2, 1865. This Battery was organized at Burlington, and left for Washington on the 15th of January, 1864, where it remained under drill until the 25th of April, and then was attached to the Ninth Army Corps, but was not engaged until they arrived opposite Petersburg, where they became active participants in the siege of that place, and Captain Start reported that in the almost daily artillery duels in which they participated, the conduct of the officers and men, amid all the dangers, hardships, and great privations of the campaign, was all that he could desire.

On the 2d of April, when the general assault was made upon Petersburg, this battery was under fire of artillery and infantry during the whole day, and officers and men, without exception, behaved as became Vermonters. Captain Start named "Lieutenants Rowell and Perrin, Sergeants William H. Parker, Parker C. Thomas, and Benjamin M. Clay, Corporals George H. Kelley, Lewis E. Gilman, and Frank F. Libby, and Private William Washburn, as deserving special mention for coolness and conspicuous gallantry during the day."

On the 3d of April Captain Start was placed in command of the reserve artillery brigade of the Sixth Corps, and directed to take charge of twenty pieces of captured artillery, and to move the brigade and captured guns to City Point, which was done, and the brigade remained in camp there until the 3d of May, when they started by way of Richmond and Fredericksburg for Alexandria, Va., where they arrived on the 18th. On the 5th of June the Battery started for Burlington, where the men were mustered out on the 13th.

First Regiment of Cavalry.

This regiment was mustered into the United States service at Burlington, on the 19th of November, and left the State with nine hundred and sixty-six officers and men on the 14th of December, 1861. It was successively commanded by Lemuel B. Platt, of Colchester, who resigned February 27, 1862; Jonas P. Holliday, of the Second United States Cavalry, who committed suicide April 5, 1862; Charles H. Tompkins, of the Fifth United States Cavalry, resigned September 9, 1862; Edward B. Sawyer, of Hydepark, resigned April 28, 1864; Addison W Preston, of Danville, killed in action at Salem Church, Va., June 3, 1864; William Wells, of Waterbury, promoted Brigadier General United States Volunteers, May 19, 1865; and Josiah Hall, of Westminster, mustered out June 21, 1865.

This regiment was in seventy-three engagements, from Mount Jackson, April 16, 1862, to that at Appomattox Court House, April 9, 1865. During the early part of their service they were engaged in picket duty in front of Washington, having detachments quartered in several different fortifications in the vicinity of that city. On the 1st of April, 1863, they were in a skirmish with Mosby's guerrillas, in which Captain Henry C. Flint, of Company I, and First Lieutenant Charles H. Woodbury, of Company B, — both brave and dashing officers, — were killed. Several enlisted men were killed and wounded in this engagement. On the 30th of May, Lieutenant Colonel Preston, with one hundred and twenty-five officers and men, and a detachment of the Fifth New York Cavalry, were sent out in pursuit of Mosby and one hundred guerrillas, who had attacked and plundered a train of cars near Kettle Run, Va., Company H, Lieutenant Hazelton, and Company C, Sergeant Hill, charged up a narrow road, in the face of a terrible storm of grape and shell. Lieutenant Colonel Preston, in his report, says, "The rebels fought their piece with desperation, firing their last shot after they were surrounded by our men, which shot passed through a horse not twenty feet from the gun, and wounded several men. Lieutenant Chapman (rebel) never left his gun, but with his revolver wounded several men in hand-to-hand fight.

He was wounded twice, and captured. Mosby fled through the woods, closely pursued, leaving his artillery and gunners in our possession. We recaptured the mail taken from the cars, and several other things, with a number of prisoners. As a feat of daring, it has not been exceeded during the war."

The Adjutant General of Vermont, in his report for 1863, says, "During the campaign in Maryland and Pennsylvania, in June and July, the regiment, under the command of Lieutenant Colonel Preston, participated in a series of engagements, in which both officers and men behaved most gallantly. At Hanover, Huntsville, Gettysburg, Hagerstown, and Boonsboro', they fought with the most reckless bravery, and won a reputation second to none. The casualties, from June 30 to July 8, were, nineteen killed and forty-four wounded."

Through July and August the regiment was constantly on the move, and had almost daily skirmishes with the enemy and with guerrillas. On the 1st of September they composed a part of the expedition into King George County, Md., which resulted in the capture of two rebel gun-boats by cavalry, and on the 3d returned to their camp near Falmouth, Va., and picketed at the Rappahannock until the 12th, when they went to Culpeper Court House, and charged through the town, driving the enemy, capturing eight prisoners and one gun, carriage, and horses. They again met the enemy in force near James City, on the 10th of October, and in the retreat from that place through Culpeper to Brandy Station and across the Rappahannock, and the attendant engagement, the regiment again distinguished itself for coolness and daring bravery, repeatedly charging the enemy, and was highly commended by the brigade commander. All through that month and November they were almost continually on the move, having frequent skirmishes with the enemy. On the 6th of December they went to Stevensburgh, where they remained until the 28th of February, 1864, picketing the line of the Rapidan.

On the 29th of February this regiment assisted in destroying the depot and railroad at Beaver Dam Station. On the 1st of March they crossed the Chickahominy, and halted three miles from Richmond. From thence they moved to Mechanicsville, having destroyed a mile of trestle-work railroad on the way. On the 4th they marched to Yorktown, from whence detachments were sent out on various expeditions of responsibility and danger. They went to Alexandria on the 13th, and from thence to Stevensburgh, where they arrived on the 18th, and remained there until the 3d of May. On the 5th they met the enemy's cavalry at Craig's Church, where a sharp fight ensued, lasting several hours, in which they lost four men killed, three officers, and twenty-four men wounded, and fourteen missing. They were again engaged at Yellow Tavern, seven miles from Richmond, five hours, driving the enemy from their position, with the loss of General Stuart, Brigadier General Gordon, and others. This regiment lost two men killed, two officers, eight men wounded, and four missing.

On the 1st of June the regiment was again engaged at Ashland, losing seven men wounded, and two officers and twenty-four men captured. Again, on the 3d, at Salem Church, in a fight with the enemy, they lost two officers killed, and five men wounded. At White Oak Swamp, on the 13th, they were engaged during the entire day, losing one killed, twelve wounded, and three missing. At Malvern Hill, on the 15th, they had one officer and two men wounded. On the 22d they went with General Wilson on his celebrated raid into the enemy's country. In a severe fight with the enemy, on the 28th and 29th, near Strong Creek Station, one officer was wounded and missing, eleven men wounded and seventy-five missing. For eleven days the regiment was marching, fighting, destroying property, and breaking the connection of the enemy. They were almost every day throughout the months of July, August, and September, on the move, fighting, skirmishing, and destroying rebel property. In

September, Colonel William Wells, who had been in command of the regiment from the 3d of June, was placed in command of the Second Brigade, and the command of the regiment devolved upon Lieutenant Colonel John W Bennett. In February, 1865, Colonel Wells was breveted Brigadier General for gallant and meritorious service, and on the 19th of May was appointed Brigadier General of Volunteers. Colonel Wells reported, that while the regiment was under his command, "the field, staff, and line officers of the regiment rendered most valuable service, and that no regiment in the Division marched more miles, or fought more battles, than the First Vermont."

On the 19th of October the regiment was again engaged with the Brigade commanded by General Custer, in a desperate fight with the enemy, displaying great coolness and courage. They captured one hundred and sixty-one prisoners, a large number of horses, wagons, and a large amount of other rebel property. Lieutenant Colonel Bennett reported that "every officer and man under his command, who participated in that charge, conducted himself with such gallantry as to merit special mention."

On the 22d of October, 1864, the original members of the regiment, who had not re-enlisted, returned to Vermont, and were mustered out on the 18th of November. They left in the field about four hundred men and three officers, under command of Major William G. Cummings. On the 20th of December the division to which the Vermont Regiment was attached, while on a reconnoissance, was attacked in camp just before daylight. The attack was made upon the Eighth New York. The First Vermont, hearing the firing, moved at once in its direction, skirmished for a while with the enemy, and then made a charge, capturing about thirty prisoners, without losing a man. On the 22d the regiment went into winter quarters near Winchester, Va., where they remained until the opening of the spring campaign. On the 1st of February, 1865, Lieutenant Colonel Josiah Hall rejoined the regiment and assumed command.

On the 27th of February the regiment broke camp, and started on the spring campaign, forming a part of General Custer's Division of General Sheridan's command, the history of the movements of which, during the closing month of the war, is well known, and will be long and gratefully remembered by the loyal people of the country. The conduct of this regiment throughout was such as any Vermonter may well be proud to remember. They were at Appomattox Court House on the 9th of April, and in line of battle while the terms for the surrender of Lee's army to General Grant were being arranged.

On the 9th of June the regiment left Washington

for Vermont, arriving at Burlington on the 13th. Those recruits whose terms of service would expire before the 1st of the next October, were mustered out of service on the 21st, and the remainder of the men were consolidated into six companies, and Lieutenant Colonel William G. Cummings placed in command, Colonel Hall having been mustered out. Two companies were stationed at St. Albans, and the others at different points in Northern New York, with headquarters at Champlain. The battalion was finally mustered out of service on the 9th of August, 1865.

The history of the marches, skirmishes, charges, and battles of the Vermont Cavalry alone would make a most thrillingly interesting book, of dimensions much larger than this one. No organization in the army, it is believed, endured more exposure and fatigue, without a murmur or complaint; fought more battles without straggling and flinching; made more desperate and successful charges into the ranks of the enemy, or deserved more honor, than the First Vermont Cavalry.

BIOGRAPHICAL.

GENERAL GEORGE J. STANNARD.

THE design of this book would not be carried out without a particular notice of Brigadier General George J. Stannard, of St. Albans. He was identified with the Vermont troops from the commencement to the close of the war. He served in several different organizations and in many capacities, from Lieutenant Colonel of the Second Vermont Regiment to commander of the First Division of the Eighteenth Army Corps, showing himself in all of them, and on all occasions, a most capable, intelligent, cool, brave, and faithful officer. To him, as much as to any single man, is due the enviable reputation which the Vermont troops obtained and enjoyed for patience, faithfulness, and soldierly conduct in camp, and gallantry on every field, during the whole four years of the great struggle of loyalty with treason.

General Stannard was born at Georgia, Franklin

County, Vermont, in 1820. He was educated in the public schools of his native town, and at the academies there and at St. Albans, with a view to a collegiate course, which he finally abandoned, and engaged as clerk in a foundery establishment at St. Albans. He subsequently became a partner in the business, and so continued until the breaking out of the rebellion.

When the Vermont Volunteer Militia was organized, in 1855, the Third Company — afterwards known as the Ransom Guards — was enlisted at St. Albans, and General Stannard was chosen First Lieutenant, which position he held until the organization of the Fourth Regiment, in 1858, when he was elected Colonel, and was the second ranking Colonel in the State.

In April, 1861, immediately after the assault upon Fort Sumter, General Stannard corresponded with the commanders of the several companies composing his regiment, and having obtained the consent of all of them, tendered his services, with his regiment, to the State to defend the flag. He made the tender by telegraph to Governor Fairbanks, and also to Brigadier General Jackman, commander of all the militia of the State. General Stannard was the first man in Vermont to volunteer for the war. His regiment was formally accepted; but later it was decided by the authorities that the first regiment from Vermont should be made up from all its Volunteer Militia, and the selection, by companies, was left with the Adjutant and Inspector General, H. H. Baxter.

On the 6th of June, 1861, General Stannard was commissioned Lieutenant Colonel of the Second Regiment Vermont Volunteers, and had charge of its organization at Burlington. Before the Second left the State, he was offered the Colonelcy of the Third Regiment Vermont Volunteers, but declined it, preferring to remain with the regiment he had been instrumental in recruiting and making ready for the field.

General Stannard was commissioned Colonel of the Ninth Regiment Vermont Volunteers, on the 21st of May, 1862, and recruited, organized, and went to the field with it. Without solicitation on his part, he was commissioned Brigadier General of United States Volunteers on the 11th of March, 1863, by Abraham Lincoln, and his commission forwarded to him. He asked for the command of the "Vermont Brigade," with which he had been connected as Lieutenant Colonel of the Seventh Regiment, but was refused, and told that that Brigade could fight well under any commander, or without any; but that the new Vermont Brigade required an officer of energy, experience, and skill at its head, and that he must take it, which he did. The "Second Vermont Brigade" was composed of the Twelfth, Thirteenth, Fourteenth, Fifteenth, and Sixteenth, all nine months regiments.

This brigade was in but one battle, that of Gettysburg, on the 1st, 2d, and 3d of July, 1863, an account of which, with the gallant conduct of this brigade and its commander, is given in another place. In this battle, near its close, General Stannard was severely wounded in the leg by an iron shrapnel ball, which caused him great suffering until removed by a surgeon an hour afterward. He would not be taken from the field until his command was relieved from their position in the front line, his wounded taken care of, and arrangements made for burying the dead, when he mounted his horse and rode to the rear with his command. For gallantry and coolness in action he was breveted Major General of United States volunteers.

In about four weeks after the battle of Gettysburg, General Stannard, having recovered from his wounds, reported for light duty In November, 1863, he was placed in command of all the forces in New York, which position he held until May, 1864. He then joined the Army of the James, under General Butler, and was ordered to the Tenth Corps, where he remained but a short time, when he was assigned to the command of a brigade in the Eighteenth Corps, and in June took command of the First Division, in which position he continued through the summer. He was in the battles of **Drury's Bluff, Cold Harbor, Petersburg,** and Chapin's Farm, and at the taking of Fort Harrison. At Cold Harbor he lost all his staff officers, two of whom were killed and four wounded. All his orderlies but one were wounded, and he was himself wounded twice, though slightly. During the battle of Chapin's Farm, September 30, he was very severely wounded in the right arm, which was afterwards amputated at the shoulder. As soon as able he came home on leave of absence.

When General Stannard had sufficiently recovered, he reported to General Dix, commander of the Department of the East, and was ordered to the northern frontier, which was then being threatened. In February, 1866, he was assigned to a position in the Freedman's Bureau, and stationed at Baltimore, where he remained until June of that year, when he was appointed United States Collector of Customs for the District of Vermont, which place he now holds, discharging its important and responsible duties with the same fidelity and energy which characterized him in field and camp.

GENERAL PETER T. WASHBURN.

No man in Vermont was more conspicuous or important to the troops from that State, during the four years' continuance of the War of the Rebellion, than Peter T. Washburn, of Woodstock, which makes a particular notice of him essential to the completeness of this book. He was born at Lynn, Mass., September 7, 1814, and when two and a half years old removed with his father to Vermont. He graduated at Dartmouth College in 1835, and was admitted to practice, as an attorney, at the December term, 1838, commenced the practice of his profession at Ludlow in January, 1839, and removed to Woodstock, in 1844, where he has since resided; and, as a lawyer, has attained a position second to that of no man now living in Windsor County, and to that of but few in the State. In 1844 he was elected Reporter of the Decisions of the Supreme Court, for which his great industry and love of the profession of law admirably fitted him, and held the office eight years. He represented the town of Woodstock in the General Assembly of Vermont in 1853 and 1854, and took a prominent position as a debater and legislator among the ablest men of the State.

General Washburn's military career commenced

many years ago. In 1837, when but twenty-five years of age, he was elected colonel of a Vermont regiment, and resigned his commission in 1841. At the breaking out of the rebellion, in 1861, but few men in Vermont were supposed to be versed in the science of war, and it was believed to be essential to the efficiency of the troops she might send to the field that they should be commanded by men who had been educated at some military institution. To this end, in April, when the first regiment was being organized, under the call of President Lincoln for seventy-five thousand volunteers for three months' service, John W. Phelps, a graduate of West Point, and a regular army officer in the Mexican war, was appointed colonel, and Peter T. Washburn, of Woodstock, lieutenant colonel, and commanded the regiment during most of the three months of its term of enlistment. For an account of his service in the field reference may be had to the record of that regiment in another part of this book.

In October, 1861, Mr. Washburn was elected Adjutant and Inspector General of the State of Vermont, in which position he continued, being re-elected each year until after the close of the war, and the completion of his reports and records, when, in 1866, he declined a further election. It was in this position that General Washburn particularly distinguished himself. His untiring industry, and great ability as an organizer, made him of incalculable value in recruiting, arming, and putting into the field the Vermont troops. He gave himself up to the work, and did everything that could be done to add to their efficiency and comfort while there, and to secure to his State its share of the glory of the war. His records were so perfectly kept, and his reports, made to the Governor from year to year, and then published, so carefully and systematically made, that not more than a score of the thirty-five thousand men who went from the State of Vermont to the war remained unaccounted for. He was emphatically the right man in the right place. There may be other men who could perform responsible public duties as well as General Washburn performed those of this position; but it is lamentably true that they are seldom sought out and called to them. His services are appreciated by officers of every grade, and by the rank and file who served in the field. The State owes him a debt of gratitude for his five years' service in time of war in the position of Adjutant and Inspector General.

GENERAL JOHN WOLCOTT PHELPS.

In consideration of his character as a man, his having been a graduate of the United States Military Academy at West Point, and served as an officer in the regular army in the war with Mexico, John Wolcott Phelps, of Brattleboro,' was commissioned by Governor Fairbanks, on the 2d of May, 1861, Colonel of the First Regiment Vermont Volunteers, sent out under the call of President Lincoln for seventy-five thousand volunteers for three months' service. He went to Fortress Monroe with the regiment, and was commander of the post. On the 27th of May, 1861, he was promoted to Brigadier General of United States Volunteers. He went on an expedition to the Gulf of Mexico, in November, 1861, and took military possession of Ship Island, Miss.; was with Commodore Farragut's fleet in forcing the opening of the Lower Mississippi, in April, 1862, and with the naval force taking possession of Forts Jackson and St. Philip, La., April 28, 1862, and of New Orleans, La., May 1, 1862, and organized the first negro troops. He was stationed at Carrolton, seven miles from New Orleans, and his camp was literally thronged with black fugitives. General Phelps formed the men of suitable age into companies, and made a requisition on General

Butler, who was in command of the Department, for arms for them, saying, that he desired to raise three regiments of Africans for the defense of the point where he was located, which was unhealthy, and his men were dying at the rate of two or three a day. General Butler directed him to employ the contrabands in and about the camp, in cutting down all the trees, &c., for the purpose of defense, and ordered the quartermaster to furnish axes and tents for the contrabands. General Phelps replied that he was willing to organize African regiments for the defense of the Government, but would not become the mere slave-driver, "having no qualification that way," and tendered his resignation, which General Butler refused to accept.

In August, 1862, General Phelps, with his reasons therefor, returned his commission to the President. Months afterwards, when circumstances compelled the Administration to adopt the very policy proposed by General Phelps, the President offered him a Major General's commission, which he would accept only on condition that it should bear date upon the day of his resignation. To this the President would not accede, as, while it would be only justice to General Phelps, it would be an implied censure of General Butler, whose conduct in the matter was approved by the Administration, though a change of policy became expedient and necessary afterwards.

By an order of the rebel government, dated August 21, 1862, General Phelps was declared an outlaw, for having "organized and armed negro slaves for military service against their masters, citizens of the Confederacy."

General Phelps was a most accomplished officer. By his constant thoughtfulness of the comfort of his men, and his peculiar mode of enforcing discipline, he was very much respected and beloved by his whole command. On resigning his commission he returned to Brattleboro', where he has since resided, enjoying the confidence and esteem of all who know him.

LIEUTENANT COLONEL CHARLES CUMMINGS.

The subject of this notice was well and favorably known throughout the State of Vermont for his many excellent qualities of head and heart. Lieutenant Colonel Cummings was born at Royalston, Mass., in February, 1821. He studied medicine, and in 1847 received the degreee of M. D. at Woodstock. He practiced his profession at Fitzwilliam, N. H., three years, but his tastes were for literary pursuits, and he abandoned his profession, and removed to Brattleboro' in 1852, connected himself with the Brattleboro' Eagle, as associate editor with Hon. B. D. Harris, and subsequently, in a similar capacity, with the Vermont Phenix, at that place. After a time he became proprietor of the Phenix, and so continued up to the time of his death.

In 1858 Lieutenant Colonel Cummings was elected Clerk of the Vermont House of Representatives, and performed the duties of the position so acceptably that he was re-elected at three subsequent sessions. He enlisted for the war as a private in Company E, Eleventh Regiment, and was chosen First Lieutenant. Before that regiment left the State, he was commissioned by the Governor Major of the Twelfth,— a nine months' regiment, — and subsequently, before leaving the State, was commissioned Lieutenant Colonel of the Sixteenth, also a nine months' regiment. This regiment formed a part of the Second Vermont Brigade, a full account of the movements of which is given elsewhere in this book. For a few months he was Provost Marshal at Fairfax, performing the duties to general acceptance.

In February, 1864, Lieutenant Colonel Cummings was assigned to the Seventeenth Regiment, and in April, not being full so that a colonel could be mustered, the regiment left the State for the seat of war under his command. In the battle of the Wilderness, on the 6th of May, 1864, during a hand-to-hand fight, in a thick wood, he was wounded in the scalp by a minie ball. His wound, together with subsequent hard service and exposure, so enfeebled him that he came home on leave of absence in August, where he remained about a month, and, before being able to do so, returned and rejoined his regiment at the front. In the engagement at Poplar Grove Church, on the 30th of September, 1864, while rallying his men, he was wounded in the thigh, fell into the hands of the enemy, and died upon the field. His last words were, "Save the colors, boys!"

From his long connection with the newspaper press as editor, where he had shown more than ordinary ability; as an officer, for four years, of the General Assembly, and in other ways, Lieutenant Colonel Cummings had become widely known and respected; and when he lost his life, gallantly battling for the right, his death was sincerely mourned throughout the State.

COLONEL JOHN STEELE TYLER.

Colonel Tyler was one of many promising young men who left pleasant and comfortable homes in Vermont, and went forth to do battle in the war of the great rebellion, and never returned. He was a son of Rev. Thomas P. Tyler, D. D., of Batavia, N. Y., and grandson of the late Hon. Royall Tyler, for sixteen years judge of the Supreme Court of Vermont. Lieutenant Colonel Tyler graduated, at the age of fifteen, at a school in Connecticut, where students were instructed and drilled in military tactics. At sixteen years of age he entered the law office of his uncle, Hon. Royall Tyler, of Brattleboro', as a student, and two years afterward, in April, 1861, enlisted as a private in Company C, Second Regiment Vermont Volunteers, and was elected First Lieutenant; promoted Captain, January 23, 1862; Major, February 9, 1853; Lieutenant Colonel, April 2, 1864, and Colonel, May 6, 1864. He died at the Metropolitan Hotel, New York City, on the 23d of May, 1864, of wounds received in the battle of the Wilderness on the 5th.

Colonel Tyler's military record in the field is identical with that of the Second Vermont Regiment, which will be found in this book. Colonel Tyler distinguished himself in his regiment for his gentlemanly and soldier-like bearing, and in many battles for his gallantry receiving the commendation of his superior officers. He left behind him many friends, who feel that this was a noble sacrifice laid upon the altar of their country.

MAJOR CHARLES JARVIS.

MAJOR CHARLES JARVIS.

Major Jarvis was the only surviving son of Hon. William Jarvis, — better known as Consul Jarvis, — of Weathersfield. He was born on the 21st of August, 1821; was mortally wounded in an encounter with the enemy near Cedar Point, N. C., December 1, 1863, and died in a few hours. His remains were brought home, and his funeral attended by a large concourse of relatives, friends, soldiers, and citizens of his own and neighboring towns, on the 13th of December, 1863. No man from Vermont who lost his life in the war of the rebellion was more generally respected for his many virtues, or more sincerely mourned by all who knew him, than was Major Charles Jarvis. He fitted for college principally at Phillips Academy, Exeter, N. H., and entered the University of Vermont at the age of fourteen, the youngest member of his class. He maintained a high standing for scholarship and deportment in college, and graduated with honor in 1839. He studied law, and graduated at the Law School in Cambridge, Mass., in 1842.

After obtaining his degree at Cambridge, at the solicitation of his aged father, who needed his assistance in the cares and responsibilities of extensive agricultural and pecuniary concerns, he decided that duty —

which he always regarded as paramount — dictated that he should remain at home. On the breaking out of the Great Rebellion, in 1861, he again felt that duty called him to the defense of the Constitution and laws of his country. When remonstrated with by his many friends and neighbors, who appreciated his worth as a citizen, and knew his importance as the head of a large family, bereft of a husband and father by the death of Consul Jarvis, in October, 1859, he replied, "There are things dearer than life," and "I had rather be a martyr to my country than live in ease at home." Soon after the breaking out of the war, he went to Washington, and tendered his services to the Government, in any capacity where he could be most useful in suppressing the rebellion.

In June, 1862, Major Jarvis recruited a full company, in his own and adjoining towns, for the Ninth Regiment, and was chosen its Captain. After some appropriate remarks, he presented each of his men a handsomely-bound Bible. He was tendered a higher position, but preferred to remain with the men who knew and appreciated him. His regiment left the State for the seat of war in July, 1862. This regiment was a part of the eleven thousand and five hundred troops disgracefully, and it was feared treacherously, surrendered by Colonel Miles, an experienced regular army officer, to Stonewall Jackson, at Harper's Ferry, on the 15th of September, 1862. They were paroled and sent to Chicago, but not exchanged until December. In June, 1863, Captain Jarvis was promoted to Major of his regiment, and was killed as stated. The commander of the regiment, Colonel Edward H. Ripley, in a letter to Major Jarvis' family, wrote, "He died gloriously, as could all hope to do, battling in a stern, inflexible vindication of the right of man to liberty — proving in death that his devotion to his country was of no ordinary intensity, and his faith in the promises of his religion unbounded. He passed away, as he had lived, a brave soldier and simple-hearted, devoted Christian, and left an example that has found its way to all our hearts, and whose impression will never fade away."

Resolutions, complimentary to the head and heart of Major Jarvis, and of condolence and sympathy for his family, were passed by the Ninth Regiment, by the Bar of Windsor County, of which he was a much respected member, and by citizens of Weathersfield.

BREVET MAJOR ELIJAH WALES.

But few men who went to the war from Vermont, or any other State, fought more battles, received a greater number of wounds, and had more hair-breadth escapes, than Brevet Major Elijah Wales, of Brattleboro', and he still lives to tell his own story. His record is a most creditable, remarkable, and interesting one. He enlisted as a private, and was mustered into Company C, Second Regiment, May 1, 1861; appointed First Sergeant, June 20, 1861; promoted Second Lieutenant, January 23, 1862; First Lieutenant, October 20, 1862; Captain, March 1, 1863; and Brevet Major, August 1, 1864, for gallantry in the Wilderness and subsequent engagements.

Major Wales participated in twenty-four battles, and says he was under fire more times than he would undertake to count. He was wounded in the battle of the Wilderness, May 5, 1864 — a minie ball entering his left shoulder-blade, passing between his heart and spine, and coming out under the right shoulder-blade, near the arm. He was in the field again in less than two months, and was wounded in an engagement at Strasburg, Va., August 4, 1864, by a minie ball, in the head, breaking the bone in over the left eye. He did not leave his regiment, but participated in a skirmish at Stony Point the fourth day afterwards, and was twice wounded, once in the wrist and again in the right leg. He served to the end of the war, was mustered out with his regiment, and was honorably discharged.

During his term of service, Major Wales performed many daring and gallant acts. At Petersburg, on the

2d of April, 1865, he, with two men, captured a piece of artillery, turned it upon the enemy, and fired upon them the charge they had themselves placed in the gun. He returned to Brattleboro' after "the cruel war was over," still resides there, and may he long live to enjoy the blessings of the good government for which he most nobly fought.

LIEUTENANT COLONEL ADDISON BROWN, JR.

Lieutenant Colonel Addison Brown, Jr., was a son of Mr. Addison Brown, of Brattleboro', one of the proprietors and editors of the Vermont Phenix. He was another of the many young men who went from Vermont to the field, and distinguished himself for gallantry in battle, and good conduct on all the trying occasions incident to the life of a soldier in time of war. When the war broke out he was living at Brooklyn, N. Y., and enlisted as a private in the Twelfth New York Regiment, under the call of the President for three months' volunteers. This regiment was the first to cross Long Bridge into Virginia, where for some time it was on duty, and afterward returned to Washington. At the end of his three months' term of enlistment, Lieutenant Colonel Brown returned to his home in Brattleboro', and immediately enlisted in Company F, Fourth Vermont Regiment. He was chosen Captain of that company, and commissioned by the Governor, September 21, 1861, and held the same position until September 18, 1864, when he was promoted to Lieutenant Colonel, and placed in command of the Fifth Vermont Regiment, which position he resigned on account of disability, December 9, 1864.

During a large share of the three years that he was captain in the Fourth Regiment, he was detailed to duty on the staff of the "Vermont Brigade," and was Assistant Inspector General through the battles of the Wilderness, when the Brigade, consisting of less than three thousand men, held their position against the assault of fourteen thousand rebels. During the first day of this engagement all the officers on the Brigade staff, except Captain Brown, were either wounded or captured, leaving him alone on the staff during the remainder of the battles of the Wilderness. The general commanding the Brigade, in his report of the affair, said, in speaking of Captain Brown, "Most nobly and gallantly he performed the duties of three officers. It was an occasion which called for unusual abilities, courage, and powers of endurance, and Captain Brown was found equal to the occasion."

At the battle of Opequan Creek, near Winchester, on the 19th of September, 1864, Lieutenant Colonel

Brown, who was in command of the Fifth Regiment again distinguished himself, and was mentioned in complimentary terms by the officer commanding the "Vermont Brigade."

After Lieutenant Colonel Brown's discharge from service, he declined in health until the 3d of March, 1865, when he died at Harrisburg, Pa. His remains were brought to Brattleboro', where his funeral was attended by a large concourse of soldiers, firemen, and citizens, all seeming anxious to pay their respects to one who,

"Leaving in battle not blot on his name,
Looks proudly to heaven from the death-bed of fame."

CAPTAIN DENNIE W. FARR,

A native of Chesterfield, N. H., and brother-in-law of Lieutenant Colonel Addison Brown, Jr., enlisted at Brattleboro', as a private, in August, 1861; was chosen Second Lieutenant of Company F, Fourth Regiment, and rose to the rank of Captain. He was one of the first men killed in the battle of the Wilderness. He was struck in the head by a minie ball when waving his sword and encouraging on his men. He was twenty-four years old, and gave up his life, which was full of hope, a willing sacrifice to his country.

INCIDENTS AND ANECDOTES.

BEFORE THE BATTLE OF BETHEL.

"JUST as we halted, to start to the rear, on hearing firing," said Adjutant Stevens, of the First Vermont, "a rebel scoundrel came out of a house, and deliberately fired his gun at us. The ball passed so near to me that I heard it whiz on its way, going through the coat and pants, and just grazing the skin of Orderly Sergeant Sweet, of the Woodstock company. The rascal is secured, and is a prisoner; and what was done, by way of stern entertainment, to one of the F. F. V.'s, you will hear if I live to return. I then, as the firing to the rear had ceased, with revolver in hand, accompanied by Fifer, approached the fellow's house, having some expectation of an ounce of lead being deposited in my tall body without asking my permission. By this time all our troops were out of sight in the woods, by a turn in the road, and I was alone with Fifer, when negroes came from the house, having less fear of two men than of two thousand. On inquiring, the slaves told us that Adjutant Whiting, whom we had just taken prisoner, was the owner; that he belonged to the secession army, and that no white folks were in the house, all having left. Without the ceremony of ringing, I entered and surveyed the premises, and found a most elegantly furnished house. I took a hasty survey in search of arms; but finding none, left the house, and started to overtake our column. On reaching the bend in the road, I took a survey of the rear, to 'see what I might see,' and discovered a single soldier coming toward me, and waited for him to come up. I found it was Clark, of the Bradford company. Before he reached me, I observed a horseman coming at full speed toward me. On reaching the house, he turned in, which induced me to think him a secessionist. I ordered Clark to cover him with his rifle, and, revolver in hand, ordered him to dismount and surrender. He cried out, 'Who are you?' Answer, 'Vermont.' 'Then raise your piece, Vermont. I am Colonel Duryea, of the Zouaves;' and so it was. His gay-looking red boys just appeared, turning the corner of the road, coming toward us. He asked me the cause of the firing in the rear, and whose premises we were on. I told him he knew the first as well as I did, but as to the last, could give him full information; that the house belonged to one Adjutant Whiting, who just before had sent a bullet whizzing by me, and shot one of my boys, and that my greatest pleasure would be to burn the rascal's house in payment. 'Your wish will be gratified at once,' said the colonel. 'I am ordered by General Butler to burn every house whose occupant or owner fires upon our troops. Burn it.' He leaped from his horse, and I upon the steps, and by that time three Zouaves were with me. I ordered them to try the doors with the butts of their guns. Down went the door, and in went we. A well-packed traveling-bag lay upon a mahogany table. I tore it open with the hope of finding a revolver, but did not. The first thing I took out was a white linen coat. I laid it on the table, and Colonel Duryea put a lighted match to it. Other clothing was added to the pile, and we soon had a rousing fire. Before leaving, I went into the large parlor in the right wing of the house: it was perfectly splendid! A large room, with tapestry carpet, a nice piano, a fine library of miscellaneous books, rich sofas, elegant chairs, with superior needle-work wrought bottoms, whatnots in the corners loaded with articles of luxury, taste, and refinement, and upon a mahogany center-table lay a Bible and a lady's portrait. The last two articles I took, and have them now in my possession. I also took a decanter of most excellent old brandy from the sideboard, and left the burning house. By this time the Zouave regiment had come up. I joined them, and in a short time came up with our rear guard, and saw a sight the like of which I wish never to see again, viz.: nine of Colonel Townsend's Albany Regiment stretched on the floor of a house, where they had just been carried, and eight of them mortally wounded *by our own men.* O, the sight was dreadful! I cried like a boy, and so did many others. I immediately thought of my decanter of brandy; took a tin cup from a soldier, and poured into it the brandy, and filled it — the cup — with water from a canteen, and from one poor boy to another I passed, and poured into their pale and quivering lips the invigorating fluid, and with my hand wiped the sweat-drops of death from their foreheads. O, how gratefully the poor fellows looked at me, as they saw, by my uniform, that the usually stern officer and commander had become to them the kind and tender-hearted woman, by doing for them woman's holy duty! One strong fellow, wounded in the head, and bloody as a butcher's floor, soon rallied, and was able to converse with me. I asked him if he knew the poor fellows around him. He said 'Yes,' and pointing to one, he said, 'that man stood at my side; he was my section-man. I saw his gun fly out of his hands, being struck by a grape-shot, and a moment after we both tumbled to the ground together.' I went out and picked up an Enfield rifle, nearly cut in two by a ball.

Said he, 'That is his gun.' I saw its owner die, and brought the gun with me back to my camp, and have it in my possession."

THE LAST WORDS OF COLONEL STONE.

Much has been said — but not too much — in praise of Colonel Newton Stone, late commander of the Second Vermont Regiment, who fell in the second day's fight in the Wilderness. He was first wounded in the leg, and conveyed to the rear; and after having his wound dressed, requested to be placed upon his horse, which was done, when he immediately rode to the front, and took his position at the head of his regiment, amid the cheers of his men, whom he addressed briefly, as follows: —

" Well, boys, this is rough work; but I have done, as I told you I wished you to do, not to leave for a slight wound, but remain just as long as you could do any good: I am here to do as long as I can." He then rode along the line, speaking a word of good cheer to every company, and as he halted to address Company B, a rifle ball pierced his head, and he fell from his horse a corpse. At that moment the regiment was forced back, and the body of their colonel was captured, but was immediately retaken.

BRAVERY AT LEE'S MILLS.

Among the incidents of the fight at Lee's Mills, Va., on the 16th of April, 1862, was the recovery from a fever of Sergeant Fletcher, of Company E, Third Vermont, on the sick list, and excused from duty, and the use he made of his temporary health. He crossed the stream and went through the fight; then, on his return, was among those who went back and rescued the wounded. On his return to camp he went into hospital, and resumed his fever, with aggravation.

John Harrington, a beardless orphan boy, of seventeen, unarmed, went over and rescued out of the rifle-pit a disabled comrade.

Lieutenant Whittemore commanded Company E. This officer, with his revolver, covered Harrington in his hazardous expedition, and killed several rebels who aimed their pieces at the boy. His most intimate friend in the company, private Vance, had been killed in the rifle-pit. Whittemore, enraged with sorrow, burst into tears, and seizing the dead soldier's musket, stood over him, and threatened death to any who should retreat; and then stooping down, he took cartridge after cartridge from his friend's box, and killed his man with every fire — raging with a divine fury the while.

Among the phenomena of the fight was the condition of the uniform of Captain Burnett, of Company K, Third Vermont. It had eight bullet holes in it, one through the collar of his coat, one through the right coat sleeve, one through his pantaloons below the left knee, one through both pantaloons and drawers above the right knee, and four through the skirts of his coat. There was not a scratch upon this man's skin.

A SLAVE'S PRAYER.

A Virginia slave, who had heard of the President's promise concerning the Proclamation to be issued on the 1st of January, then only a few days in the future, was heard praying with great earnestness and a deeply-affected heart, thus: —

"O, God Almighty! keep the engine of the rebellion going till New Year's! Good Lord! pray don't let off the steam; Lord, don't reverse the engine; don't back up; Lord, don't put on the brakes! But, pray, good Lord, put on more steam! Make it go a mile a minute! Yes, Lord, pray make it go sixty miles an hour!" "Amen! Do, good Lord!" responded the brethren and sisters. "Lord, don't let the express train of rebellion smash up till the 1st of January! Don't let the rebels back down, but harden their hearts as hard as Pharaoh's, and keep all hands going, till the train reaches the Depot of Emancipation!"

ESCAPED PRISONERS.

A noticeable thing about the war is the fact that the colored people of the South were, without an exception, friendly to the Union cause, and aided and abetted the Union army in every way in their power — which, from their intimate knowledge of the country, was much greater than many people suppose. When trusted by our men in distress they never betrayed them. They took tender care of sick and wounded Union soldiers whenever they fell into their hands, and in multitudes of instances aided prisoners in escaping from Andersonville, Salisbury, and other hells, where they were confined to suffer torture, starvation, and death. They concealed them by day in their cabins and other secure places, and piloted them on their way to our lines by night. Many an escaped prisoner owes his life to the men and women of that oppressed race.

ESCAPE OF UNION SOLDIER.

A DYING SOLDIER PRAYS FOR PRESIDENT LINCOLN.

Never, until we stood by the grave of the Green Mountain boy, did we realize how much stranger is truth than fiction. A private was court-martialed for sleeping on his post, out near Chain Bridge, on the Upper Potomac. He was convicted; his sentence was death. The finding was approved by the general, and the day fixed for his execution. He was a youth of more than ordinary intelligence. He did not beg for pardon, but was willing to meet his fate.

The time drew near. The stern necessity of war required that an example should be made of some one. His was an aggravated case. But the case reached the ears of the President; he resolved to save him; he signed a pardon and sent it out. The day came. "Suppose," thought the President, "my pardon has not reached him." The telegraph was called into requisition. An answer did not come promptly. "Bring up my carriage," he ordered. It came, and soon important state papers were dropped, and through the hot, broiling sun, and over dusty roads, he made his way to the camp, about ten miles, and saw that the soldier was saved.

He had doubtless forgotten the incident, but the

soldier had not. When the Third Vermont charged upon the rifle-pits the enemy poured a volley upon them. The first man who fell was William Scott, of Company K, with six bullets in his body. His comrades caught him up, and, as his life-blood ebbed away, he raised to Heaven, amid the din of war, the cries of the dying, and the shouts of the enemy, a prayer for the President; and, as he died, he remarked to a comrade that he had shown he was no coward, and not afraid to die.

He was interred in the presence of his regiment, in a little grave about two miles to the rear of the rebel fort, in the center of a group of holly and vines. A few cherry trees, in full bloom, are scattered around the edge. In digging his grave a skull and bones were found, and metal buttons: showing that the identical spot had been used, in the Revolutionary War, for our fathers who fell in the same cause. The chaplain narrated the circumstances to the boys, who stood around with uncovered heads. He prayed for the President, and paid the most glowing tribute to his noble heart that we ever heard. The tears started to their eyes as the clods of earth were thrown upon him in his narrow grave, where he lay shrouded in his coat and blanket.

The men separated; in a few minutes all were engaged in something around the camp, as though nothing unusual had happened; but that scene will live upon their memories while life lasts. The calm look of Scott's face, the seeming look of satisfaction he felt, still lingered; and, could the President have seen him, he would have felt that his act of mercy had been wisely bestowed.

ANECDOTES.

A LIEUTENANT was promenading in full uniform one day, and approached a volunteer on sentry, who challenged him with "Halt! Who comes there?" The Lieutenant, with contempt in every lineament of his face, expressed his ire with an indignant "Ass!" The sentry's reply, apt and quick, came, "Advance, ass, and give the countersign."

During the march of McClellan's army up the Peninsula from Yorktown, a tall Vermont soldier got separated from his regiment, and was trudging along through the mud endeavoring to overtake it. Finally, coming to a crossing, he was puzzled as to which road he should take; but, on seeing one of the "natives," his countenance lighted up at the prospect of obtaining the desired information, and he inquired, "Where does this road lead to?" "To h—l," was the surly answer of the "native." "Well," drawled the Vermonter, "judging by the lay of the land, and the appearance of the inhabitants, "I kalkerlate I'm most thar."

The day before Grant attacked Fort Donelson, the troops had had a march of twenty miles, part of it during a bitter cold night. Grant called a council of war, to consider whether they should attack the fort at once, or should give the troops a day or two's rest. The officers were in favor of resting. Grant said nothing until they had all given their opinion; then he said, "There is a deserter come in this morning. Let us see him, and hear what he has to say." When he came in, Grant looked into his knapsack. "Where are you from?" "Fort Donelson." "Six days' rations in your knapsack, have you not, my man?" "Yes, sir." "When were they served out?" "Yesterday morning." "Were the same rations served out to all the troops?" "Yes, sir." "Gentlemen," said Grant, "troops do not have six days' rations served out to them in a fort if they mean to stay there. These men mean to retreat, not to fight. We will attack at once."

HEROISM AT FREDERICKSBURG.

Captain James H. Platt, Jr., of Company B, Fourth Vermont Regiment, having been ordered with his company to the right of the skirmish line, after having once expended nearly all his ammunition and been resupplied, led his men out in front of a battery, within three hundred yards, where they did noble execution till a charge of cannister struck down half the company, killing four and wounding fourteen, when he ordered them back to re-form, which they did, and retired in good order with the regiment just relieved. Yet not all: for, calling some to his side, the humane captain, a skillful physician, bound up the most dangerous wounds, thus prolonging at least several lives, and, with the assistance he had summoned, bore away to the hospital, a mile distant, all who were unable to help themselves. This was done amid bullets flying like hail; yet, through a kind Providence, no one was harmed. As the gallant captain said, "God would not let us suffer while in discharge of such a duty."

THE DRUMMER BOY.

Willie Johnson, thirteen years old, of St. Johnsbury, a drummer boy in Company D, Third Vermont Regiment, received a medal for his heroic conduct in the seven days' fight before Richmond. On the retreat, when strong men threw away their guns, knapsacks, and blankets, that they might have less weight to carry, this little fellow kept his drum, and brought it safely to Harrison's Landing, where he had the honor of drumming for division parade, being the only drummer who brought his drum from the field. When these facts were reported to the War Department by the division commander, Willie was presented with a star medal of honor by Secretary Stanton in person.

DON'T SEE IT.

The following instance is given of Vermont pluck: In Kilpatrick's last "On to Richmond" was a soldier-boy by the name of Edwin A. Porter, whose mother lives in Wells, Vt. In one of the skirmishes, he rode up fearlessly to a squad of rebels. The officer demanded of him to surrender. He replied, coolly, "Don't see it;" and, suiting his action to his words, he instantly drew his saber, with which he cleft the head of the officer, at the same instant wheeling his horse to join his company, the rebels firing a volley at him, of which shower the lad carried off in his person four bullets, joining his company, G. He kept his saddle for more than an hour, and finally recovered from his wounds, and was discharged February 17, 1865.

www.ingramcontent.com/pod-product-compliance
Lightning Source LLC
Chambersburg PA
CBHW030748250426

43672CB00028B/1347